POTATO
KITCHEN

Manuela Rüther

POTATO KITCHEN

Contents

Preface

*Out of the cellar and
into the kitchen.*

Potatoes were an ever-present feature of my childhood on the farm. Barely a day went by when they were not served up in one form or another. Sometimes we got mashed, jacket, or boiled potatoes. Other days we might get chips or potato croquettes. Often potatoes were the central attraction, perhaps in a creamy casserole or savoury tart; sometimes we got a hearty helping of fried potatoes with bacon, onions, and fried eggs; other times it was simple potato fritters with apple purée.

As a child, I never questioned this abundance of potatoes. After all, they were always absolutely delicious. What's more, from my child's perspective, I never considered chips, potato fritters, and gratin to be repetitive. Quite the opposite! And I found nothing surprising about the fact that all these delicious things could be made from one and the same root vegetable.

Potatoes themselves seemed equally unremarkable to me. They just grew in the garden. In spring we would plant them out with Grandpa Fritz; and in the autumn we would fetch

in the harvest, usually during what were referred to as the "potato holidays". Ringing in our ears would be Granny's enigmatic motto "The stupidest farmers grow the fattest potatoes", which my little sister would chant and repeat till the cows came home because it amused her so much.

I never gave a second thought to the incredible variety of potatoes or their different flavours. It just never occurred to me. Why would it? Unlike apples, our potatoes all looked pretty similar: they were oval, brown, and covered in soil. After washing, they were brownish yellow, and after peeling, they were even yellower. They looked like potatoes in other words. In terms of taste, some were floury, others were waxier. And their names? Anya, Charlotte, or Desirée – many were women's names, all similar. I wonder why?

Luckily, my attitude would gradually change. Certainly by the time I was training as a chef, I had grown to appreciate the incredible diversity offered by this vegetable. Heritage potatoes would turn up in the kitchen, varieties with different names, shapes, and colours, and each with its own distinctive taste. The French gourmet variety La Ratte celebrated a comeback on menus in exclusive restaurants. Blue mash became all the rage. The Linda was brought back from near extinction in Germany. Eventually, other varieties would be too.

But it was not just gourmet chefs who were realizing the potential of the potato. Gradually, this vegetable was also winning over the hearts and minds of amateur chefs for everyday cooking. Food markets began to stock far more than the standard floury or waxy varieties. Vendors would sing the praises of the creamy Blue Congo or Blue Anneliese, which is particularly good for making mash. Or they might extol the virtues of the Red Emmalie. In summary, at the start of the 21st century, the potato had emerged from its dark cellar to become a culinary star once again.

And it has maintained this status – quite rightly so and to our enormous delight. While working on this book, the potato took us on a global culinary voyage. So often we found ourselves sitting in the photo studio marvelling at the amazingly delicious recipes we had discovered. Not a single day of shooting went by without at least four different potato dishes being served up: from colourful potato canapés to hearty stews or spicy potato salads and Malaysian potato curry, from hash browns to chips or Hasselback potatoes, from savoury tarte tatin to sweet and fluffy potato soufflé with vanilla pears. Whether the dishes were salty or sweet, rustic and savoury, vegetarian or vegan, local or international, our conclusion was that no cookbook could possibly capture the full potential of the potato. But it was still worth a try! Join us as we explore the world of the potato.

The recipes

One more thing about the recipes: you might wonder why I introduce so many types of potatoes but then only mention the desired cooking characteristics in the recipes. This is because there are too many varieties, all of which vary in terms of availability year by year and depend on your location. Also the cooking characteristics are much more important than the precise flavour for the success of a recipe. It does not make any sense to stipulate a specific variety for a particular dish. It's much better to try things out for yourself and find your own favourite variety for each occasion. You will find all sorts of options at food markets, farm shops, and online.

I hope you enjoy!

Ela

INTRODUCTION

The potato, a local cosmopolitan – field trips from Peru to Europe

A trip to Peru…

Of course, everyone knows that Sir Walter Raleigh did not actually discover the potato. What children learn at school is that he is said to be responsible for introducing this root vegetable to Britain in the late 16th century. Needless to say, potatoes originally come from South America. Everyone knows that!

Even so, it's amazing to see this vegetable in Peru. There it is, dotted colourfully across fields high up in the Andes and piled up in the incredible markets between plucked chickens and cow's heads. One market trader after another sells just this crop: potatoes in all sorts of shapes and colours. They might look a bit different from the potatoes back home (more colourful, much more bulbous, stranger shapes) and they taste different too (more intense, less sweet, and with a waxier texture), but they are nonetheless unmistakably the same.

There is much to learn about the history of the potato around the Peruvian city of Cuzco, the centre of the advanced Inca culture, and in the Andes mountains. The Incas cultivated more than 3,500 varieties of potato in South America between the 13th and 16th centuries.

Today, dedicated potato enthusiasts are collaborating with local farmers to preserve and recultivate as many heritage varieties as possible. The potato has a sacred status for the Quechua, the indigenous population around Cuzco. They feel a sense of responsibility for its preservation. Since as early as 1971, there has been a potato research centre in Lima (Centro Internacional de la Papa), which collects and preserves genetic material from potato varieties from several South American countries. About an hour away from Cuzco, in the Sacred Valley of the Incas, you will also find the Parque de la Papa, a park dedicated to the potato. More than 12,000 hectares (29,650 acres) have been assigned to growing countless different potato varieties. It is a unique project with the world's most diverse collection of potatoes.

Not only in Peru but also across the entire Andes region, the potato is one of the most important foodstuffs for the often very poor rural population. Potatoes are one of the few plants that can grow at more than 4,000 metres (13,000 feet) and thrive in these harsh conditions. It is not known exactly where the potato originated from. Traces of the oldest wild potatoes go back 13,000 years to the Chiloé Island, off the coast of Chile. But today's potatoes probably come from different varieties cultivated in the Andes, from western Venezuela south to Argentina.

... into history...

So the question is, how did the potato get to Europe from South America? And how did it manage to establish itself so successfully? First the disappointing news: nobody knows exactly who introduced this root vegetable. In the late 16th century, English sailors, such as Sir Walter Raleigh, brought this plant with its lovely flowers home with them. Earlier still, the Spanish conquistadors had introduced it to the Spanish mainland via the Canary Islands. The potato then reached Italy, from where it gradually spread throughout the rest of Europe. In Italy, it was initially confused with the truffle, a fungus that grows underground, so some people called it by the same name – "*tartufulo*" or "*tartufo*". This term comes from the Latin *terrae tuber*, which means, roughly, "tuber of the earth".

However, this exotic plant did not exactly enjoy a triumphal procession in Europe to begin with. Aristocrats and botanists admired the *Solanum tuberosum* for its lush foliage and beautiful flowers. But its main use was as an ornamental plant in botanical gardens rather than as an arable crop. It was only the failed harvests, famines, and wars in Europe in the 17th and 18th centuries that heralded the start of potato farming. Various European rulers recognized the vegetable's potential and tried to introduce legislation encouraging its cultivation. Among them was Frederick the Great of Prussia with his potato laws. Peter the Great was another, introducing potatoes to Russia. But rural people were sceptical. There was no information about how to prepare the vegetable, so people ate it raw, unsuccessfully, and sometimes even consumed its poisonous foliage. What's more, the Church frowned upon the potato as food for "savages" – in other words, the non-Christian population of South America. The fact that potatoes were not mentioned in the Bible and that they grew underground were other factors that counted against them. Potatoes were regarded as the devil's work.

So, how did they succeed against such opposition? Their success was mostly due to persistent food shortages and the fact that farmers recognized that this new plant could produce higher yields than wheat, for example. Potatoes were also easy to cultivate. The soil requirements were not particularly demanding, and farmers could harvest them using simple tools. Storage and preparation were also straightforward. And this fantastic root vegetable turned out to be a vital staple food thanks to its valuable constituents, particularly carbohydrate and high-quality protein, but also dietary fibre and important vitamins and minerals, such as B vitamins, vitamin C, potassium, calcium, phosphorus, and magnesium.

The same is true today. With more than 7,000 different varieties and an annual harvest of about 370 million tonnes (408 million tons), the potato is one of the world's most important staple foods. Nowadays, potatoes are grown almost everywhere in the world, from America and Europe to Russia and Asia. The United Nations (UN) declared 2008 to be the International Year of the Potato to promote awareness of the significance of this precious food, particularly in developing countries. According to the UN, the potato has great potential in terms of protecting food security for the world's population.

... and back to earth

Unless a potato variety is suitable for mass cultivation, however, it can soon be threatened with extinction, which would gradually lead to a disappointing monotony in the world of the potato. Over recent years, though, there has been a renewed appreciation for quality and flavour. The Bamberg potato, one of the oldest varieties of potato in Germany, almost died out at one point because it wasn't suitable for mass cultivation and the yields were too low. The same fate almost befell the Linda. Activists campaigned vigorously, and these varieties were brought back from the brink.

Many other heritage varieties have similar stories to those of the Linda and Bamberg. Some potatoes have profited so much from this renewed interest that they have become highly sought after. The French variety La Bonnotte is one such example. It is grown only on the island of Noirmoutier in the Bay of Biscay. Soil plays a crucial role in the flavour of a potato, and it's the sandy soil, naturally enriched with seaweed, that gives this highly prized potato its very special, slightly salty flavour. After almost disappearing completely, it's now one of the most coveted – and expensive – varieties in the world.

In the UK, although almost 1,200 potato varieties are held in the government's reference collection in Scotland, only about 80 varieties are grown commercially. It is worth cooking a few different types in their skins and having a tasting session to give you an understanding of the nuances in flavour, which are often far more interesting than those of your average supermarket spud. You quickly realize what is missing in mass-cultivated produce.

Sourcing, storing, and cooking

Farm shops and farmers' markets can be a great source for less well-known and heritage varieties. Online suppliers delivering nationwide include the Morghew Park Estate in Kent (morghew.com) and Natoora (natoora.co.uk). Vegetable box subscriptions such as those from Abel & Cole (abelandcole.co.uk) or a local greengrocer or wholesaler may also include more unusual tubers.

Some suppliers choose to leave the soil on their potatoes before they're sold as washing makes them more delicate and can cause them to deteriorate faster. Store potatoes in a cool, dark, well-ventilated place and wash them just before cooking to help them last longer. It's worth buying a vegetable bag with a blackout lining to help keep your potatoes fresh.

For success in the kitchen, the cooking characteristics are more important than the flavour. In the UK, potatoes are generally classified as floury or waxy. Floury varieties have a high starch content and more "dry matter". This gives a fluffy interior, making them ideal for jacket or roast potatoes, chips, and mash. Waxy varieties have dense, smooth flesh that won't fall apart when cooked, so leave them whole or chop, slice, or even grate them into recipes. Some potatoes fall in between the two poles: they hold their shape when boiled but can still be mashed. These all-rounders include Desirée, Wilja, and Estima.

So, let's explore the surprising versatility and flavour spectrum of the potato – it's high time to get cooking and tasting!

POTATO
VARIETIES

Waxy potatoes

JERSEY ROYAL

The famous Jersey Royal is grown only on the
Channel Island of Jersey, where a combination
of the unique microclimate and light, well-
drained soil creates the perfect conditions for
it to flourish. These much-lauded potatoes enjoy
Protected Designation of Origin (PDO) status.
Harvested from April to June, they have a
characteristic sweet, nutty flavour and are
best served boiled and anointed with butter.

BLUE ANNELIESE

Developed in 2007 in Germany, this late-ripening
waxy variety is known for its creamy flavour,
nutty, chestnut-like aroma, and unmistakable
deep-purple skin and flesh. Try it in salads or
use it to make blue mash – be sure to leave the
skin on to retain the colour. It is available from
specialist suppliers.

PINK FIR APPLE

A fingerling variety, these distinctive tubers
are known for their pale pink skin and narrow,
knobbly shape. Imported from France in 1850,
they're still harvested by hand owing to their
unusual form. With its firm flesh and earthy,
nutty flavour, the Pink Fir Apple is ideal in
salads or roasted whole and served with nothing
more than a drizzle of good olive oil and a
sprinkling of sea salt.

RED EMMALIE

Bred in Germany from the waxy La Ratte and
the more floury Highland Burgundy Red, the
texture of this striking red-fleshed potato sits
somewhere between the two, making it useful
in a range of dishes. With its aromatic, slightly
floral flavour, it is perfect baked into gratins or
boiled with the skin on.

MARIS PEER

This light, fresh-tasting variety is ideal in salads, and its firm texture also makes it perfect for boiling or steaming. Look out for smaller tubers that don't require peeling.

LA RATTE

This firm, yellow-fleshed variety is known for its subtle hazelnut or chestnut flavours. First cultivated in France in the 19th century, these small fingerling potatoes have recently been repopularized and are available in some supermarkets and specialist shops. Since they hold their shape well, they're typically left whole and boiled or steamed, then added to salads or casseroles. French chefs use La Ratte to make a smooth mash despite its waxy texture: the late Joël Robuchon specified it for his famous butter-laden pomme purée.

CHARLOTTE

The most popular salad potato in the UK, it has a light brown skin that is thin enough to leave on. Try them simply boiled or steamed or slice them into a gratin dauphinois.

ANYA

This relatively new salad potato dating from the 1990s was bred in Scotland from the Pink Fir Apple and Desirée and named after Lady Sainsbury. It's a second early, meaning it crops in the middle of the season, about July to August. Deep-set eyes give the thumb-sized Anya a dimpled appearance, while the dense, creamy flesh has a slightly nutty flavour. Try it in salads where its thin skin can be left on.

See overleaf for images ▶

Waxy potatoes

JERSEY ROYAL

BLUE ANNELIESE

PINK FIR APPLE

RED EMMALIE

MARIS PEER

LA RATTE

CHARLOTTE

ANYA

Floury potatoes

VITELOTTE

Known as the truffle potato in Germany, the elongated Vitelotte is small and bulbous, with a delicately nutty and aromatic flavour similar to the chestnut. With its unique purple marbling and dark, rough skin, this floury variety makes the most amazing-looking gnocchi. It is available from specialist suppliers.

MAYAN GOLD

The first potato in the UK to be bred from wild Peruvian varieties, this rich golden oval tuber is considered by some to be the perfect roasting potato. Intensely flavoured with a texture that's both creamy and fluffy, it's well worth tracking down. What's more, it's said to cook in half the time of standard spuds.

SHETLAND BLACK

As the name suggests, this heritage variety hails from the Shetland Islands, where it was first bred in 1923. The pale yellow flesh is ringed with purple while the skin is almost black. To retain its distinctive appearance and sweet, buttery flavour, try roasting it in wedges or slicing into crisps for frying.

KING EDWARD

First grown in 1902 and named after the reigning British monarch at the time, Edward VII, this cream-coloured potato with light red blushes is another popular choice. It is perfect for roast, baked, and jacket potatoes.

MARIS PIPER

A British favourite since it first appeared in the 1960s, this is the workhorse of the potato world. It's great for chips and roast potatoes, as well as mash and wedges, and is widely available throughout the UK.

HIGHLAND BURGUNDY RED

This Scottish heritage variety was reportedly served to the Duke of Burgundy at the Savoy in London in 1936 to add some colour to his meal, picking up its name in the process. Beneath the bright red skin of these oval potatoes, the floury red flesh is ringed with white. To retain the vibrant hue, keep the skin on: you'll be rewarded with fluffy pink mash, deep red roasties, and sensational rustic crisps.

POTATO VARIETIES

26

VITELOTTE

MAYAN GOLD

KING
EDWARD

SHETLAND
BLACK

HIGHLAND
BURGUNDY RED

MARIS PIPER

Cooking characteristics

WAXY POTATOES

These contain very little starch – 14 per cent on average. Some varieties have a creamy, firm consistency, making them ideal for salads or simply boiling. When cut, the surface is slightly shiny. Try them in recipes where you need potatoes to hold their shape, such as casseroles, hash browns, potato fritters, Hasselback potatoes, potato spirals, and gratins.

CHARLOTTE

ANYA

BLUE ANNELIESE

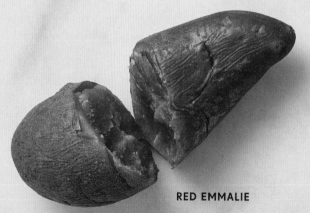

RED EMMALIE

FLOURY POTATOES

These contain relatively high levels of starch, around 16.5 per cent, which causes them to break down when cooked. They have a fluffy, coarse, soft, and dry texture. The skin may burst open during boiling. They are suitable for making chips and roast potatoes, and are perfect for mashed potato, purées, dumplings, gnocchi, potato noodles, croquettes, and thickening soups.

MARIS PIPER

HIGHLAND BURGUNDY RED

MAYAN GOLD

SHETLAND BLACK

STARTERS
AND
SNACKS

This classic Asian starter is given the fusion cuisine treatment with potatoes and sauerkraut, adding a European touch.

Spring rolls with sauerkraut, potatoes, and a sweet and sour sauce

Vegan
Serves 4
Preparation 15 minutes
Cook 20 minutes

For the sauce
1 garlic clove
2 tbsp brown sugar
100ml (3½fl oz) apple juice
3½ tbsp rice vinegar
5 tsp soy sauce
1 tsp tomato purée
1 heaped tsp cornflour
salt and freshly ground
    black pepper

For the spring rolls
2 waxy or floury boiled
    potatoes (prepared
    previously)
200g (7oz) fresh sauerkraut
1 red or green chilli
    (according to taste)
1 tsp coriander seeds
1 tsp nigella seeds
1 tsp raw cane sugar
neutral-tasting vegetable oil
    for frying (such as
    rapeseed, sunflower,
    or groundnut)
12 spring roll wrappers

To make the sauce, peel and finely chop the garlic, then sauté it in a pan with the sugar. Add the apple juice, vinegar, soy sauce, and tomato purée and simmer for 5 minutes over a moderate heat. Mix the cornflour with 1–2 tbsp cold water, stir this into the sauce, and bring to the boil. Season the sauce to taste with salt and leave to cool.

Peel and dice the potatoes and transfer them to a bowl. Drain the sauerkraut thoroughly, chop roughly, and add to the potatoes. Slice the chilli in half lengthways, remove the seeds, and chop. Grind the coriander seeds with a pestle and mortar. Add both these ingredients to the bowl along with the cumin and sugar, mix well, and season with salt and pepper.

Meanwhile, add 3–4cm (1¼–1½in) of oil to a deep frying pan and heat to a temperature of 160–170°C (320–340°F). Spread the spring roll wrappers out on a work surface with the

corners towards the edge of the counter. Put 2 tsp of filling in the centre of each sheet, then brush the edges with a small amount of water. Fold the corners at each side over the filling, then roll up the wrappers from bottom to top. Fry the spring rolls in batches in the hot oil for 2–3 minutes each until golden, then drain on kitchen towel. Arrange the spring rolls on a plate, sprinkle with salt, and serve with the sauce.

Tip: this is a fantastic recipe for using up leftover potatoes, and their cooking characteristics do not particularly matter. If you don't want to fry the spring rolls, you can also bake them in the oven at 180°C (160°C fan/ 350°F/Gas 4) for 20–25 minutes until golden.

Chutney, here in the form of an onion jam, is a great way to spice up lots of dishes. Here it makes the perfect complement to these creamy and filling Swabian ravioli.

Swabian potato ravioli with mushrooms, cheese, and onion jam

Vegetarian
Serves 4
Preparation 20 minutes
Cook 30 minutes

For the onion jam
300g (10oz) onions
3 tbsp brown sugar
100ml (3½fl oz) red wine
3½ tbsp red wine vinegar
1 bay leaf
2 cloves
1 star anise
salt and freshly ground
    black pepper

For the potato ravioli
600g (1lb 5oz) floury
    potatoes
300g (10oz) mushrooms (e.g.
    button, porcini, shiitake,
    chanterelles, oyster, or
    king oyster)
50g (1¾oz) butter
75g (2½oz) Emmental
    or Gruyère
2 sprigs of rosemary
50g (1¼oz) full-fat
    cream cheese
1 egg yolk
150g 00-grade plain flour,
    plus extra for working
grated nutmeg
5 tbsp neutral-tasting
    vegetable oil

Special equipment
potato ricer

To make the onion jam, peel and halve the onions, then slice thinly. Add the onions, sugar, wine, vinegar, bay leaf, and spices to a saucepan and bring to the boil over a high heat. Then simmer and thicken over a low heat for about 20 minutes, stirring occasionally. Season the jam with salt and pepper and leave to cool.

Peel and chop the potatoes, then boil in lightly salted water for about 20–25 minutes until soft. Meanwhile, wash and dab dry the mushrooms, trim if necessary, and chop. Heat half the butter in a frying pan and sauté the mushrooms until golden. Season with salt and pepper. Grate the cheese. Wash and shake dry the rosemary, strip the leaves from the stalks, and chop. Combine the cooled mushrooms with the grated cheese, cream cheese, and rosemary, then season well with salt and pepper.

Pour away the potato cooking water and let the potatoes steam for 1 minute, then process them twice through a potato ricer while they are still hot. Add the egg yolk, flour, ½ tsp salt, 2–3 pinches of nutmeg and the remaining butter and mix everything together with a wooden spoon. Do not knead this mixture or it will go sticky – it should have a dry consistency. If in doubt, work in some additional flour.

Roll out the potato dough on a floured work surface to about 30 x 30cm (12 x 12in). Slice in half across the centre. Put half of the filling on each strip of dough, leaving a gap around the edge. Roll up the dough from the long side, pressing it together along the edges. Use a floured wooden spoon handle to divide this into roughly 3cm- (1¼in-) wide parcels. Seal the sides.

Heat the oil over a moderate heat in a non-stick pan and fry the ravioli parcels for 2–3 minutes on each side until brown. Serve these Swabian ravioli with the onion jam. Lamb's lettuce goes beautifully with this dish.

A fantastic recipe for a party, these kebabs are easy to make and taste absolutely delicious. Use smallish potatoes that are about the same size.

Colourful potato kebabs with garlic yogurt

Vegetarian
Serves 4
Preparation 15 minutes
Cook 25 minutes
Marinating 1 hour

For the potato kebabs
4 purple waxy potatoes
4 yellow waxy potatoes
salt and freshly ground
    black pepper
1 tsp caraway seeds
4 sprigs of thyme
2 sprigs of sage
1 sprig of rosemary
4 tbsp olive oil
2 small courgettes
50g (1¾oz) green and black
    olives, pitted and drained
12 wooden skewers

For the dip
2 garlic cloves
300g (10oz) full-fat
    natural yogurt
juice of ½ lemon

Wash the potatoes and boil for 15–20 minutes in lightly salted water flavoured with caraway seeds. Meanwhile, wash and shake dry the herbs. Strip the leaves from the stalks and chop. Combine the herbs with the oil and 2 pinches of salt and pepper. Drain the potatoes, peel, then slice into halves or quarters and marinate in the herby oil while still warm. Cover and leave the flavours to develop at room temperature for 1 hour.

Peel and finely chop the garlic for the dip. Mix the garlic, yogurt, and lemon juice. Season with salt and pepper.

Wash the courgettes, trim, and discard the ends. Slice the courgettes in half lengthways, chop into 2cm (³/₄in) pieces, add to the potatoes, and toss in the oil. Slide alternate pieces of potato, olives, and courgette onto the wooden skewers.

Heat a frying pan over a high heat and fry the kebabs. Press down slightly while cooking to make sure the courgettes take on some colour. Season the kebabs with salt and pepper and enjoy while hot or lukewarm. Serve the dip alongside.

Tip: if you like, you can slide some ham onto the kebabs between the potato and courgette.

Soft, sweet dates wrapped in salty, crispy bacon – this is a classic and hugely popular dish. Walnuts add a bitter note in this version. In combination with potatoes and crisp sesame seeds, the result is a very sophisticated tapas dish.

Potatoes wrapped in bacon with a date stuffing

Serves 4
Preparation 15 minutes
Cook 45 minutes

8 medium waxy potatoes
salt and freshly ground
    black pepper
4 dried dates, pitted
50g (1¾oz) walnuts
½ bunch of thyme
8 slices smoked bacon
3 tbsp olive oil
3 garlic cloves
1 tbsp sesame seeds, toasted

Wash the potatoes, then boil in lightly salted water for about 20–25 minutes until soft. Meanwhile, roughly chop the dates and walnuts. Wash and shake dry the thyme. Strip the leaves from four sprigs.

Drain the potatoes and slice in half lengthways. Using a teaspoon, scoop out the potato halves into a bowl, aiming to leave a roughly 1cm- (¹/₂in-) thick shell. Mix the scooped-out potato filling with the dates, nuts, and thyme leaves, then season with salt and pepper. Preheat the oven to 240°C (220°C fan/475°F/Gas 9).

Fill the scooped-out halves of potato with the date and walnut mixture and put the halves back together. Wrap each potato with a slice of bacon, transfer to a baking dish, and drizzle with oil. Slice the unpeeled garlic cloves in half and scatter these between the potatoes along with the remaining thyme. Bake the potatoes for 20 minutes until crisp, remove from the oven, sprinkle with sesame seeds, and serve hot.

Tip: any leftover filling tastes great with some salad or served as a warm mash.

This colourful platter is guaranteed to be a hit at any buffet.
Try out each version in turn at home to save time.

Potato canapés

Serves 6–8
Preparation 10 minutes
Cook 25 minutes

For the potatoes
10 medium waxy potatoes
salt and freshly ground
 black pepper
1 tsp caraway seeds

Wash the potatoes carefully and boil for 20–25 minutes in lightly salted water flavoured with caraway seeds. Drain the potatoes, leave to cool, and then peel. Before serving, slice two potatoes for each recipe variation into 1cm- ($^1/_2$in-) thick slices, season with salt and pepper, then garnish as follows.

Smoked salmon and horseradish

1 sprig of dill
1 tsp sesame seeds
1 piece of fresh horseradish
 (roughly 2cm/¾in)
4 slices smoked salmon
4 tsp creamed horseradish
 sauce (from a jar)

Wash the dill, shake it dry, strip the leaves, and chop finely. Toast the sesame seeds in a dry pan until golden. Grate the fresh horseradish.

Top the slices from two potatoes with smoked salmon and garnish each with a dollop of horseradish sauce. Sprinkle with dill, sesame seeds, and grated horseradish before serving.

Cheese spread and speck

6 radishes
3–4 tbsp cheese spread
4 thin slices of speck or
 other ham, cut in half
2 tsp fried onions
freshly ground black pepper

Wash, trim, then thinly slice the radishes. Spread the slices from two potatoes with cheese spread and top with radish, ham, fried onions, and freshly ground black pepper.

Liver pâté and redcurrants

1–2 sprigs of chervil
4 stems of redcurrants
1 tsp redcurrant jelly
1 pinch of chilli flakes
75g (2½oz) coarse liver pâté

Wash the chervil and shake dry, then strip off the leaves. Wash the redcurrants, strip the berries from the stalks, and combine with the jelly and chilli flakes.

Spread the pâté over the slices from two potatoes. Top with the marinated berries and garnish with chervil.

Pea purée and marinated asparagus

Vegan
2 white asparagus spears
1 tsp za'atar
grated zest and juice of ½
    organic lemon
salt and freshly ground
    black pepper
1 tbsp olive oil
1 small garlic clove
100g (3½oz) frozen peas,
    defrosted
1 handful of pea shoots

Special equipment
hand-held blender

Peel the asparagus and discard the woody ends. Thinly slice the asparagus spears and marinate with the za'atar, lemon zest, 2 pinches of salt, and oil. Peel the garlic. Use a hand-held blender to finely purée the peas and garlic with the lemon juice, 2 pinches of salt, and some pepper. Spread the purée over the slices from two potatoes. Top with asparagus and pea shoots.

Pickled herring and apple

2 pickled herring fillets
½ red apple
1 shallot
juice of ½ lemon
salt and freshly ground
    black pepper
1 tsp green peppercorns
2 tbsp chopped chives

Dice the pickled herring. Wash and core the apple, then dice it finely including the skin. Peel and dice the shallot. Combine the herring, apple, and shallot in a bowl. Add the lemon juice, a dash of salt, and some black pepper, then spread over the slices from two potatoes. Roughly chop the green peppercorns and scatter these with the chives over the canapés.

Popular in southern Germany but completely unknown in the north, this is a fantastic dip or sandwich spread that you really should try. It is a classic recipe to use up leftover potatoes from the previous day, but you can, of course, cook the potatoes specifically for this recipe.

Potato spread – a savoury sandwich filling

Vegetarian
Serves 4–6
Preparation 10 minutes
Cook 5 minutes

3 garlic cloves
3 tbsp olive oil
1 bunch of flat-leaf parsley
1 red onion
3 floury boiled potatoes
    (prepared previously)
150ml (5fl oz) sour cream
1 tsp ground caraway seeds
salt and freshly ground
    black pepper
hot paprika (optional)

Peel and thinly slice the garlic. Heat the oil in a pan and sauté the garlic. Meanwhile, wash and dab dry the parsley, strip off the leaves, and chop. Remove the garlic from the pan and drain on kitchen towel.

Peel and dice the onion. Peel and dice the potatoes, then combine thoroughly with half the diced onion, sour cream, and caraway to create a spreadable mixture.

Season with salt and pepper. Sprinkle the potato spread with parsley, garlic, and the remaining chopped onion before serving. Dust with hot paprika if desired.

Tip: if you don't like sautéed garlic, you can use fried onions as a topping instead. This potato spread is the ideal portable food for picnics or barbecues.

This simple potato dish is a variation on Spanish patatas bravas – fried diced potatoes with a spicy sauce – as served in every tapas bar. This slightly less spicy version makes an ideal lunch or supper.

Patatas with salsa

Vegan
Serves 4
Preparation 15 minutes
Cook 45 minutes

For the potatoes
1kg (2¼lb) small
    waxy potatoes
1kg (2¼lb) coarse sea salt

For the salsa
1 onion
3 garlic cloves
4 large vine tomatoes
2 tbsp olive oil
2 tbsp chopped almonds
1 tsp smoked paprika
½ tsp hot paprika
2 tsp brown sugar
1 tsp dried oregano
juice of ½ lemon
salt and freshly ground
    black pepper
1 bunch of flat-leaf parsley

Special equipment
hand-held blender

Preheat the oven to 180°C (160°C fan/350°F/Gas 4). Wash the potatoes. Spread half the sea salt in an ovenproof dish, add the potatoes on top, cover with the remaining sea salt, and bake for 45 minutes.

Peel and dice the onion and garlic for the salsa. Wash and halve the tomatoes, remove the stalks, and dice the flesh. Heat the oil in a pan over a low heat and gently sauté the onion, garlic, and almonds for 3–4 minutes. Add both types of paprika, the sugar, and oregano, and sauté briefly. Next, add the tomatoes and lemon juice, season the salsa with salt and pepper, and simmer uncovered for 10 minutes. Finally, use a hand-held blender to purée the salsa but leave a little texture.

Wash the parsley and shake dry. Chop the leaves and the stalks and stir these into the salsa shortly before serving. Serve the salsa with the potatoes.

Tip: you can easily prepare the salsa in advance and leave the flavours to develop in the fridge overnight. It can be eaten warm or cold.

SOUPS
AND
STEWS

Potato soup is a traditional dish that is popular in many parts of the world, and there are countless different versions. This classic potato soup is thick with a dill and cream topping.

Classic potato soup with sour cream

Vegetarian
Serves 4
Preparation 15 minutes
Cook 25 minutes

For the soup
500g (1lb 2oz)
    floury potatoes
2 carrots
¼ celeriac bulb
1 onion
½ leek
olive oil for frying
salt
1 pinch of granulated sugar
100ml (3½fl oz) white wine
1 litre (1¾ pints) vegetable
    stock
3 sprigs of marjoram
200ml (7fl oz) single cream
1 pinch of grated nutmeg

For the topping
1 bunch of dill
200ml (7fl oz) sour cream

Special equipment
hand-held blender

Peel and dice the potatoes, carrots, celeriac, and onion. Trim and wash the leek, then slice into rings. Heat some oil in a large frying pan. Add the chopped ingredients and sauté over a moderate heat. Sprinkle in a pinch of salt and sugar, allow to caramelize briefly, then deglaze the pan with the wine. As soon as the wine has simmered off, pour in the stock. Add the marjoram to the soup and cook the vegetables for about 20 minutes until soft.

To make the topping, wash the dill and shake dry. Set aside a few sprigs for garnish. Strip the leaves from the remaining stalks, chop finely, mix into the sour cream, and season with salt.

Remove the marjoram from the soup and pour in the single cream. Use a hand-held blender to blend the soup, then season with nutmeg and salt.

Serve in deep soup bowls topped with a dollop of dill cream and garnished with the reserved sprigs of dill. This soup tastes great with a fresh country loaf or toasted baguette.

Hearty potato stew with sausages

Serves 4
Preparation 15 minutes
Cook 40 minutes

1 large onion
2 garlic cloves
400g (14oz) waxy potatoes
2 carrots
2 parsnips
2 sticks celery
¼ Savoy cabbage
2 sprigs of rosemary
2 sprigs of sage
2 sprigs of thyme
olive oil for frying
salt and freshly ground
    black pepper
1 tsp honey
100ml (3½fl oz) white wine
500ml (16fl oz) vegetable
    stock
1 tsp mustard
1 dash Worcestershire sauce
3 spring onions
1 bunch of chives
8 Frankfurters

Peel and dice the onion and garlic. Peel the potatoes, carrots, and parsnips, wash the celery, and dice all these vegetables. Wash the Savoy cabbage, remove the stalk, and chop into rough strips. Wash the herbs and shake dry. Strip the leaves and chop.

Heat some oil in a large frying pan and sauté all the vegetables except the cabbage over a moderate heat for a few minutes. Add the herbs, salt, and honey, then deglaze the pan with wine. Simmer off the wine, then add the stock and 500ml (16fl oz) water. Simmer the soup uncovered for 30 minutes, adding the Savoy cabbage after 20 minutes.

Season to taste with salt, pepper, mustard, and Worcestershire sauce. Wash, trim, and slice the spring onions and chives into rings. Add both to the soup with the sausages. Heat for 5 minutes but do not allow the soup to boil. Serve with rye bread and butter, making sure there are two Frankfurters in each bowl of soup.

Tip: this is a delicious family meal that does not take long to make, and it tastes even better the next day.

The head chef at the Ritz-Carlton in New York is said to have invented this chilled potato soup in the early 20th century, naming it after the French town of Vichy, near where he grew up. Here this classic dish is given a Mediterranean twist with garlic, olive oil, and lemon juice.

Vichyssoise with a crispy spring onion topping

Vegetarian
Serves 6
Preparation 15 minutes
Cook 30 minutes
Chill 2 hours

For the soup
500g (1lb 2oz)
    floury potatoes
3 shallots
3 garlic cloves
2 leeks
5 tbsp olive oil
salt and freshly ground
    black pepper
1 pinch of granulated sugar
100ml (3½fl oz) white wine
500ml (16fl oz) vegetable
    stock
100ml (3½fl oz) single cream
150ml (5fl oz) sour cream
juice of ½ lemon

5 slices day-old white bread
olive oil for frying and
    marinating
4 spring onions
sea salt

Special equipment
hand-held blender

Peel and dice the potatoes, shallots, and two cloves of garlic. Trim and wash the leeks, then slice into rings. Heat 1 tbsp oil in a large frying pan. Sauté the vegetables over a moderate heat, season with salt and sugar, then deglaze the pan with wine. As soon as the wine has simmered off, add the stock and 500ml (16fl oz) water, then simmer the soup for 20 minutes. Add the single cream, bring the soup back to the boil briefly, then use a hand-held blender to blend it. Leave to cool and chill for at least 2 hours.

Meanwhile, remove the crusts from the bread and chop into cubes. Heat some oil in a non-stick pan and fry the cubes of bread over a moderate heat until golden brown on all sides. Transfer the croutons to kitchen towel and leave to cool.

Wash and finely slice the spring onions. Marinate with pepper, sea salt, and 1 tbsp oil. Peel and chop the remaining garlic clove and add to the cold soup along with the sour cream and the remaining 4 tbsp oil. Stir this through using the hand-held blender, then season to taste with salt, pepper, and lemon juice. Serve the soup in bowls or glasses and sprinkle with croutons and spring onions.

Tip: it is essential to check the seasoning in this chilled soup because it does not have as much flavour as a hot soup. If you like, you can add some chopped herbs such as rosemary, thyme, or sage.

The flavour of this soup can be varied by using different types of cress. For example, green shiso cress gives it a minty flavour, while red shiso cress has hints of cinnamon and anise. Rocket cress, by contrast, introduces surprisingly nutty and peppery notes.

Potato and courgette soup

Vegetarian
Serves 4
Preparation 10 minutes
Cook 30 minutes

4 medium courgettes
250g (9oz) floury potatoes
1 onion
3 garlic cloves
a few sprigs of thyme
    and oregano
olive oil for frying
salt and freshly ground
    black pepper
1 pinch of ground coriander
juice and zest of ½
    organic lemon
500ml (16fl oz) vegetable
    stock
100ml (3½fl oz)
    double cream
1 punnet of cress of your
    choice (such as salad cress
    or watercress)

Special equipment
hand-held blender

Wash, trim, and finely chop the courgettes, setting aside one third for later. Peel and dice the potatoes, onion, and garlic. Wash the herbs and shake dry. Strip the leaves and chop finely.

Heat some oil in a large frying pan. Sauté the vegetables and herbs over a moderate heat. Season with salt, pepper, and coriander, then deglaze the pan with lemon juice and stock. Simmer the soup for 20 minutes, then use a hand-held blender to blend it.

Before serving, briskly fry the remaining courgette cubes and season with salt and pepper. Reheat the soup. Whip the cream until stiff and stir this into the soup along with the lemon zest.

Adjust the seasoning, then sprinkle diced courgette and cress over the soup to serve.

Tip: this is the perfect soup to use up surplus courgettes from your vegetable patch.

You could hardly get a more colourful or healthier recipe. The vegetables stay crunchy and fresh, spices supply a warming element, lemon juice creates a balanced and aromatic fresh flavour, and the lentils introduce some welcome added protein.

Colourful vegetable and potato soup with pumpernickel triangles

Vegetarian
Serves 4
Preparation 10 minutes
Cook 45 minutes

For the soup
500g (1lb 2oz) waxy potatoes
2 carrots
2 parsnips
2 beetroots
2 garlic cloves
1 leek
olive oil for frying
salt and freshly ground
    black pepper
1 tsp ras-el-hanout
½ tsp or less harissa
juice of ½ lemon
500ml (16fl oz) vegetable
    stock
500ml (16fl oz) beetroot juice
100g (3½oz) beluga lentils

For the pumpernickel
1 bunch of flat-leaf parsley
1 bunch of garden herbs
150g (5½oz) full-fat
    cream cheese
5 slices pumpernickel
    or rye bread

Peel and dice the potatoes, carrots, parsnips, and beetroots. Peel and finely chop the garlic. Trim and wash the leek, then slice into rings.

Heat some oil in a large frying pan and sauté the chopped ingredients, stirring occasionally. Add the salt, ras-el-hanout, harissa, and lemon juice, then pour in the stock and beetroot juice. Add the lentils, bring to the boil, and simmer for 35 minutes. Season to taste with salt and pepper.

Wash the parsley and garden herbs, shake dry, strip the leaves, and chop finely. Stir half the garden herbs into the cream cheese, then spread this over the sliced pumpernickel or rye bread. Stack up the slices of bread and cut into triangles or squares.

Scatter the soup with the remaining herbs and serve with the pumpernickel or rye triangles.

In northern Germany, a variety of sausage called "Pinkel" is traditionally eaten with kale. This smoked sausage contains pork fat, oat or barley groats, suet, lard, onions and spices. Every butcher has their own closely guarded recipe.

Potato and kale hotpot with bacon and smoked sausage

Serves 4
Preparation 10 minutes
Cook 30 minutes

400g (14oz) streaky bacon
800g (1¾lb) floury potatoes
4 carrots
1 large onion
1kg (2¼lb) kale
1 tbsp lard
500ml (16fl oz) vegetable
    stock
salt and freshly ground
    black pepper
1 pinch of grated nutmeg
4 smoked pork sausages
mustard to taste

Roughly chop the bacon. Peel the potatoes and cut into quarters or eighths, depending on their size. Peel and dice the carrots and onion. Chop the kale.

Melt the lard in a large frying pan and fry the bacon on both sides. Add the onion and continue cooking for a few minutes. Then stir in the potatoes, carrots, and kale. Add the stock and 500ml (16fl oz) water and season the hotpot with salt, pepper, and nutmeg. Cover and simmer

for another 15 minutes. Add the smoked sausages, continue simmering for 10 minutes, then add mustard to taste.

Tip: serve this hotpot with rye bread and mustard. If you like, you could add some pearl barley and cook this with the other ingredients.

Potato and squash are a match made in heaven. Here they are complemented by a topping made from fruity pears and tangy blue cheese.

Squash and potato soup with pear

Vegetarian
Serves 4
Preparation 15 minutes
Cook 40 minutes

800g (1¾lb) Hokkaido squash
200g (7oz) floury potatoes
1 onion
1 garlic clove
salt and freshly ground
    black pepper
1 tbsp curry powder
1 tsp ground coriander
1 tsp ground cumin
juice and grated zest of
    2 organic oranges
juice and grated zest of
    1 organic lemon
1 tsp honey
4 tbsp olive oil, plus extra
    for frying
4 pears
100g (3½oz) blue cheese
500ml (16fl oz) vegetable
    stock
thyme, to garnish

Special equipment
hand-held blender

Preheat the oven to 200°C
(180°C fan/400°F/Gas 6).
Wash the squash, remove the
seeds, and cut into 2cm- (³/₄in-)
thick slices. Peel the potatoes,
onion, and garlic, and cut into
slices or strips. Spread everything
over a baking tray and season
with salt, pepper, curry powder,
coriander, and cumin. Sprinkle
with orange and lemon zest.
Drizzle over the juice of 1
orange and the lemon, the
honey, and oil. Mix everything
well and bake for 30 minutes
in the oven.

Meanwhile, peel, core, and dice
the pears. Heat some oil in a
frying pan and fry the pears.
Roughly chop the cheese.

Add the roasted vegetables to
a pan with the stock, the juice
of the other orange, and 700ml
(1¹/₄ pints) water. Use a hand-
held blender to purée, bring
to the boil, and adjust the
seasoning. If the soup is too
thick, add a little more liquid.
Sprinkle fried pear and blue
cheese over the soup and serve
garnished with thyme.

Tip: you could also add
some ham or fried bacon
to the topping.

SALADS

Potato salad can be made with or without mayonnaise.
This is a classic recipe with home-made mayo, eggs, smoked
sausage, and pickled gherkins, just like Granny used to make.

Granny's potato salad with home-made mayonnaise

Serves 4

Preparation 25 minutes

Chill a few hours or
overnight, plus 2 hours

Cook 25 minutes

For the salad
1kg (2¼lb) waxy potatoes
salt and freshly ground
    black pepper
3 eggs
2 shallots
1 small jar pickled gherkins,
    about 190g (6¾oz) drained
    (reserve some brine)
150g (5½oz) smoked sausage
1 bunch of parsley
1 bunch of chives

For the dressing
1 large egg yolk
2 tsp lemon juice
1 tbsp mustard
100ml (3½fl oz) vegetable oil
150ml (5fl oz) sour cream
brine from the pickled
    gherkins
1 pinch of granulated sugar

Wash the potatoes, then boil in lightly salted water for about 20–25 minutes until soft.

Meanwhile, cook the eggs for 8 minutes until hardboiled, then peel and refrigerate.

Drain the potatoes and peel while still hot, leave to cool, and transfer to the fridge for a few hours or overnight.

To make the salad dressing, you first need to prepare the mayonnaise. In a tall container, stir the egg yolk, a splash of lemon juice, and mustard until smooth. Gradually whisk in the oil, drop by drop at first and then in a thin stream. Combine the mayonnaise with the sour cream and some brine from the pickled gherkins. Season the dressing to taste with sugar, salt, pepper, and lemon juice.

Dice the potatoes and eggs. Peel the shallots and dice these along with the gherkins and sausage. Transfer everything to a large bowl. Wash the parsley and chives and shake dry. Strip the parsley leaves from the stalks and chop finely. Finely slice the chives. Add both to the bowl.

Fold the dressing into the potato salad and leave the flavours to infuse in the fridge for at least 2 hours. Before serving, check the seasoning and add more salt, pepper, and possibly some brine from the pickles if desired.

Tip: if you are short of time, you can use shop-bought mayonnaise for the dressing. But there's no denying this salad tastes best with home-made mayo.

*This is the classic option for a potato salad without mayonnaise.
You can serve it lukewarm or cold and it is quick and easy to prepare.
The quality of the ingredients is vital – use a good-quality mild
vinegar, a fine oil, and richly flavoured stock.*

Potato salad with vinegar and oil

Vegan
Serves 4
Preparation 20 minutes
Marinate 1 hour
Cook 25 minutes

1kg (2¼lb) waxy potatoes
salt and freshly ground
   black pepper
1 onion
3 tbsp neutral-tasting oil,
   such as grapeseed
1 tbsp cider vinegar
1 tsp strong mustard
1 pinch of sugar
300ml (10fl oz) vegetable
   stock
1 bunch of flat-leaf parsley

Wash the potatoes, then boil
in lightly salted water for about
20–25 minutes until soft.
Meanwhile, peel and dice the
onion. Heat 1 tbsp oil in a small
saucepan and sauté the onion
until translucent. Remove from
the hob. Combine the onion,
vinegar, mustard, sugar, salt,
pepper, stock, and the remaining
2 tbsp oil to make a marinade.

Drain the potatoes, peel
while still warm, and slice
thinly, then transfer immediately
to a bowl and toss in the
marinade. Leave the salad for
at least 1 hour for the flavours
to develop, adding more stock
if necessary. The salad should
be moist.

Before serving, wash the parsley
and shake dry. Strip the leaves
from the stalks, chop finely, and
mix with the salad. Season the
salad with salt and pepper.

Tip: you can make a more
substantial, non-vegan salad
by frying finely diced bacon with
the onions and using meat stock
instead of vegetable stock,
ideally home-made of course.
This salad is delicious served
with meatloaf.

SALADS

When it comes to summer potato salads, you can let your imagination run wild. The flavours in this recipe have a southern European feel.

Mediterranean potato salad with tomato, olives, and rocket

Vegan
Serves 4
Preparation 20 minutes
Cook 20 minutes

For the salad
800g (1¾lb) small
   waxy potatoes
salt and freshly ground
   black pepper
1 red onion
300g (10oz) cherry tomatoes
½ jar sun-dried tomatoes
   in oil, about 75g (2½oz)
   drained
½ jar dried black olives,
   pitted, about 70g (2¼oz)
50g (1¾oz) rocket
a few sprigs of flat-leaf
   parsley

For the dressing
1 garlic clove
1 sprig of rosemary
1 sprig of thyme
1 sprig of sage
2–3 tbsp white balsamic
   vinegar
1 tsp Dijon mustard
1 pinch of granulated sugar
4 tbsp olive oil

Wash the potatoes, then boil in lightly salted water for about 15–20 minutes until soft.

Meanwhile, peel and finely chop the garlic for the dressing. Wash the herbs and shake dry. Strip the leaves and chop finely. Put the garlic and herbs in a large bowl and combine with the vinegar, mustard, a pinch of salt, pepper, sugar, and oil.

Drain the potatoes, leave to cool slightly, peel, and slice. Then add them to the dressing while still lukewarm and combine.

Peel the onion and slice into fine rings. Wash and halve the cherry tomatoes. Drain the sun-dried

tomatoes and cut into strips. Combine the onion, olives, and fresh and dried tomatoes with the salad, and season to taste.

Before serving, wash the rocket and dry it in a salad spinner. Wash the parsley and shake dry. Strip the leaves and chop finely. Fold both these ingredients into the salad and serve immediately.

Tip: if you don't want to eat all the salad in one go, keep it in the fridge without the cherry tomatoes and rocket. Add both these ingredients just before you are ready to serve.

Potatoes are becoming very much on trend, and this summer bowl with a crunchy hazelnut topping is a great example. Best of all, it is quick to make, the ingredients are widely available, and it won't break the bank.

Summer bowl with potatoes, beetroot, cucumber, and gherkins

Vegan
Serves 4
Preparation 20 minutes
Cook 20 minutes

For the bowl
800g (1¾lb) small
    waxy potatoes
salt and freshly ground
    black pepper
1 cucumber
4 cooked beetroots,
    vacuum packed
1 small jar pickled gherkins,
    about 190g (6¾oz) drained
1 shallot
2 spring onions
3 tbsp hazelnuts

For the vinaigrette
1 shallot
2 tbsp white balsamic
    vinegar
1 tbsp Dijon mustard
3 tbsp olive oil

Wash the potatoes, then boil in lightly salted water for about 15–20 minutes until soft.

Meanwhile, peel the shallot for the vinaigrette, dice it finely, and combine with the vinegar, mustard, and oil. Season with salt and pepper.

Drain the potatoes, peel while still warm, quarter, then transfer immediately to a bowl and dress with the vinaigrette. Wash the cucumber, and dice the cucumber and beetroots so they are slightly smaller than the quartered potatoes. Finely chop the pickled gherkins. Peel the shallot and wash the spring onions, and slice both into rings. Toast the hazelnuts in a dry pan, then chop.

Divide the potatoes between four bowls, arrange the other ingredients on top or alongside, and sprinkle with toasted hazelnuts to serve.

Potatoes and mayonnaise are a dream combination, which is why this salad has made such a triumphal procession from Moscow all over Europe. It is said to have been invented by a certain Lucien Olivier for the Hermitage restaurant in the late 19th century. This version uses yogurt in the mayonnaise dressing, making it slightly lighter.

Olivier salad

Serves 4–6
Preparation 20 minutes
Chill a few hours or
   overnight, plus 2 hours
Cook 25 minutes

For the salad
1kg (2¼lb) waxy potatoes
salt and freshly ground
   black pepper
3 eggs
3 shallots
1 small jar pickled gherkins,
   about 190g (6¾oz) drained
   (reserve some brine)
150g (5½oz) smoked sausage
   or cooked ham
1 small cucumber
1 small tin carrots and peas,
   about 265g (9½oz) drained
2 bunches of dill

For the dressing
200g (7oz) mayonnaise
100g (3½oz) full-fat
   natural yogurt
2 tsp mustard
brine from the pickled
   gherkins

Wash the potatoes, then boil in lightly salted water for about 20–25 minutes until soft. Drain the potatoes and peel while still warm. Leave to cool for a few hours or overnight in the fridge. Cook the eggs for 8 minutes until hardboiled, then peel and refrigerate.

To make the dressing, combine the mayonnaise, yogurt, and mustard, and stir in some brine from the gherkins until you have a smooth consistency. Season with salt and pepper.

Dice the potatoes and eggs. Peel the shallots and dice these along with the gherkins and sausage or ham. Wash and dice the cucumber. Drain the carrots and peas. Wash the dill and shake dry. Set some aside for garnish and finely chop the rest. Put all the ingredients in a large bowl, add the dressing, and toss.

Chill the salad for at least 2 hours and adjust the seasoning before serving with salt, pepper, and optionally some more brine from the gherkins. Garnish with the dill you set aside earlier.

Tip: this salad tastes particularly good the next day. Just check the seasoning and add more salt, pepper, and fresh dill if needed.

Potatoes taste fantastic all year round – and in summer they make a beautiful dish for a barbecue or picnic combined with creamy and tangy goat's cheese, juicy apricots, and crunchy hazelnuts.

Potato and lentil salad with apricots and baked goat's cheese

Vegetarian
Serves 4
Preparation 25 minutes
Cook 45 minutes

For the salad
800g (1¾lb) small
    waxy potatoes
salt and freshly ground
    black pepper
150g (5½oz) beluga lentils
500g (1lb 2oz)
    cherry tomatoes
8 apricots
3 spring onions
2 handfuls of rocket
3–4 sprigs of thyme
100g (3½oz) hazelnuts
250g (9oz) roll of soft
    goat's cheese
2 tbsp honey

For the dressing
4 tbsp balsamic vinegar
7 tbsp olive oil

Wash the potatoes, then boil in lightly salted water for about 15–20 minutes until soft. Drain, peel, and leave to cool.

Cook the lentils in lightly salted water for 30 minutes until just done. Drain and leave to cool.

Wash the tomatoes, apricots, and spring onions. Halve the tomatoes, remove the stones from the apricots, and slice into wedges. Finely chop the spring onions into rings. Roughly chop the potatoes and combine them with the lentils and chopped ingredients in a bowl.

Preheat the oven to 220°C (200°C fan/425°F/Gas 7). Meanwhile, wash the rocket and shake dry. To make the dressing, mix the vinegar and oil with salt and pepper. Set both aside. Wash the thyme and shake dry, strip the leaves, and chop.

Put the nuts on a baking tray and roast in the oven. Remove and chop roughly. Line the tray with baking paper. Cut the goat's cheese roll into 1.5cm- (⁵/₈in-) thick slices and place them on the tray. Drizzle with honey and scatter with thyme and pepper. Bake for 8–10 minutes until the cheese is golden.

Add the rocket and dressing to the salad and fold everything together. Scatter the toasted nuts over the salad and serve with warm baked cheese.

Tip: this tastes great with fresh or toasted baguette. For a picnic or barbecue, you can prepare the cheese in advance.

You can buy wild herbs as a ready-made salad mix. Of course, in spring you can collect your own delicious herbs or combine a shop-bought salad with wild herbs, such as dandelion greens, yarrow, daisies, wood sorrel, and so on.

Wild herb potato salad with cauliflower and smoked trout

Serves 4
Preparation 25 minutes
Cook 40 minutes

600g (1lb 5oz) small, colourful waxy potatoes
salt and freshly ground black pepper
1 small cauliflower
6 tbsp olive oil, plus extra for frying
1 pinch of curry powder
1 pinch of turmeric
1 pinch of ground coriander
2 pinches of granulated sugar
juice of 1 organic lemon
4 spring onions
1 tbsp sesame seeds
1 tbsp black sesame seeds
125g (4½oz) smoked trout fillets
150g (5½oz) wild herbs

Wash the potatoes, then boil in lightly salted water for about 15–20 minutes until soft. Drain, leave to cool slightly, peel, and leave to cool completely.

Wash the cauliflower and dab dry, then split into small florets. Heat some oil in a frying pan and fry the cauliflower, tossing it frequently until golden brown. Sprinkle with the spices and add 1 pinch each of salt and sugar. Then deglaze the pan with 1 tbsp lemon juice and 3½ tbsp water. Continue cooking until the liquid has boiled away and the cauliflower is al dente. Leave to cool.

To make the dressing, combine the remaining lemon juice with the oil, salt, pepper, and 1 pinch of sugar. Wash, trim, and slice the spring onions into rings. Toast both kinds of sesame seeds in a dry pan. Break up the trout fillets into rough chunks. Wash the salad leaves and shake dry, tearing them into bitesize pieces if necessary.

Transfer the potatoes, spring onions, and cauliflower to a bowl and add the dressing. Season with salt and pepper. Arrange the wild herbs on a platter or in a shallow dish and serve the potato salad and fish on top.

Tip: this salad is excellent with cottage cheese and crackers or wholemeal bread.

This salad packs in all sorts of flavours with its combination of sweet, salty, sharp, bitter, and sour components. It tastes best if freshly prepared.

Spiced potato salad with cucumber, yogurt, and dukkah

Vegetarian
Serves 4–6
Preparation 30 minutes
Cook 40 minutes

800g (1¾lb) floury potatoes
freshly ground coarse sea
    salt and black pepper
1 tsp harissa powder
1 pinch of ground cumin
1 pinch of nutmeg
1 pinch of dukkah (North
    African spice mix)
5 tbsp olive oil, plus extra
    for drizzling
150g (5½oz) jalapeños
1–2 garlic cloves
1 cucumber
1 bunch of flat-leaf parsley
200g (7oz) full-fat
    natural yogurt
1 tbsp tahini
juice of 1 lemon
1 tsp honey
3 shallots
1 small radicchio
100g (3½oz) hazelnuts
80g (2¾oz) dates, stoned
100g (3½oz) Kalamata
    olives, pitted

Preheat the oven to 200°C (180°C fan/400°F/Gas 6). Line a baking tray with baking paper. Peel and halve the potatoes, place them on the tray, sprinkle with salt, harissa powder, cumin, nutmeg, and dukkah, then drizzle with 4 tbsp oil and bake for 25–30 minutes. Wash the jalapeños, season with salt and pepper, and add to the potatoes after 10 minutes.

Meanwhile, peel and finely chop the garlic. Wash the cucumber, scoop out the seeds with a spoon and discard. Grate the remaining cucumber flesh. Wash the parsley and shake dry. Strip the leaves and chop finely. Combine half the parsley with the garlic, cucumber, yogurt, and tahini, and flavour with a dash of lemon juice, the remaining 1 tbsp oil, honey, salt, and pepper.

Peel the shallots and slice into rings. Wash the radicchio and shake dry, remove the stalk, and tear into bitesize pieces.

Roast the nuts for 8–10 minutes in the oven until golden brown, then chop. Slice the dates into rings.

Crush the still-lukewarm potatoes with a fork and arrange them on a shallow plate. Sprinkle the jalapeños, shallots, dates, nuts, olives, and remaining parsley over the top and put the cucumber and yogurt dip in the middle. Sprinkle the salad with sea salt and drizzle with lemon juice and oil. Serve immediately.

Tip: you can easily make your own supply of dukkah. Toast 2 tbsp fennel seeds, 2 tbsp caraway seeds, 7 tbsp coriander seeds, and 5 tbsp sesame seeds in a dry pan until they become fragrant. Grind the toasted spices with a pestle and mortar with 1 tsp anise, 1 tsp ground paprika, 3 tsp sea salt, and 2 tbsp black peppercorns. Store the mixture in an airtight container in a dark place.

Uncooked marinated asparagus is the perfect foil for boiled potatoes, and tarragon adds a sweet and tangy flavour. Other garden vegetables, such as baby peas, blanched runner beans, or raw courgette, also work well with asparagus.

Potato salad with green and white asparagus, tarragon, and prawns

Serves 4
Preparation 15 minutes
Cook 30 minutes

500g (1lb 2oz) waxy potatoes
salt and freshly ground
    black pepper
1kg (2¼lb) white asparagus
500g (1lb 2oz) green
    asparagus
1–2 sprigs of tarragon
1–2 tsp lemon juice
½ tsp or less honey
1 tsp mustard
2 tbsp olive oil, plus extra
    for frying
8 uncooked prawns, peeled

Peel the potatoes, then boil in lightly salted water for about 20–25 minutes until soft. Drain, leave to cool, and chop finely.

Peel the white asparagus and discard the woody ends. Peel the bottom third of the green asparagus spears and discard the woody ends. Slice both types of asparagus thinly and transfer to a bowl. Wash the tarragon and shake dry, strip the leaves, and chop finely. Set the stalks aside.

Dress the asparagus with salt, pepper, some lemon juice, honey, mustard, and oil. Fold in the potatoes and tarragon, adjust the seasoning, and divide the salad between four glasses or small bowls.

Heat some oil in a frying pan with the tarragon stalks and briskly fry the prawns on both sides over a high heat. Lower the heat, season the prawns with salt and pepper, and continue tossing them in the pan until they are cooked. Arrange the prawns on top of the potato salad and serve immediately.

Tip: you can also serve this salad without the prawns as a side dish to accompany grilled meat or fish.

Potatoes, green beans, and feta are a popular combination in Greece. There are a few other ingredients in this quick salad recipe, but feel free to adapt it as you prefer. You can use red or white radishes, and there is an endless variety of salad leaves to choose from.

Garden lettuce with potatoes, beans, red onions, and herbs

Vegetarian
Serves 4
Preparation 20 minutes
Cook 35 minutes

For the salad
600g (1lb 5oz) small
   waxy potatoes
salt and freshly ground
   black pepper
300g (10oz) fresh peas,
   podded
600g (1lb 5oz) runner beans
1 round lettuce
2 red onions
1 bunch of radishes
   with greens
a few stalks of marjoram
½ bunch of flat-leaf parsley
½ bunch of chervil
200g (7oz) feta

For the dressing
2 tbsp cider vinegar
1 tbsp balsamic vinegar
1 tbsp mustard
6 tbsp olive oil

Wash the potatoes, then boil in lightly salted water for about 15–20 minutes until soft. Drain, leave to cool, and peel.

In a large saucepan, bring a generous quantity of lightly salted water to the boil and blanch the peas for 3 minutes, scooping them out with a slotted spoon. Cook the beans in the same water for 8 minutes, then drain. Leave the peas and beans to cool on a shallow plate.

Remove the stalk from the lettuce, wash the leaves, and dry them in a salad spinner. Peel the onions and slice into fine rings. Wash the radishes and dab dry. Remove any wilted leaves, then

finely chop the rest. Slice the radishes. Wash the marjoram, parsley, and chervil, shake dry, strip the leaves, and chop roughly. Slice the potatoes.

To make the dressing, combine the vinegars with mustard and oil, then season with salt and pepper. Put all the prepared ingredients on a plate or in a bowl, crumble over the feta, and drizzle with some of the dressing. Serve the remaining dressing alongside.

Tip: this salad tastes fantastic with freshly baked bread and salted butter. Try it with the potato and spelt bread on p164.

Bread crisps are a popular snack that make a fantastic alternative to traditional croutons – and not just with salad. Along with the bacon, they provide a crunchy contrast to the creamy dressing.

Lamb's lettuce with potato dressing, crispy bacon, and egg

Serves 4
Preparation 20 minutes
Cook 35 minutes

For the dressing
200g (7oz) floury potatoes
salt and freshly ground
    black pepper
200ml (7fl oz) vegetable
    stock
4 tbsp vinegar
3 tsp Dijon mustard
1 pinch of granulated sugar
8 tbsp oil

For the crisps
½ wholemeal baguette
olive oil

For the salad
250g (9oz) lamb's lettuce
100g (3½oz) smoked bacon
4 eggs
2 shallots

Special equipment
potato ricer
hand-held blender

Wash the potatoes and boil in lightly salted water for 20–25 minutes until soft.

Meanwhile, preheat the oven to 200°C (180°C fan/400°F/ Gas 6). Line a baking tray with baking paper. To make the crisps, thinly slice the baguette and lay the slices over the tray, drizzle with oil, and season with salt. Bake for 10 minutes, then leave to cool.

Drain the potatoes, mash them with a potato ricer, and leave to cool. To make the dressing, use a hand-held blender to purée the potatoes, stock, vinegar, mustard, sugar, and the oil. If the dressing is too thick, add a little more stock. Season with salt and pepper.

Wash the lamb's lettuce and shake dry, discarding any damaged leaves. Finely dice

the bacon and fry in a frying pan without oil until golden brown. Depending on their size, cook the eggs for 6–8 minutes; they should have a relatively soft-boiled consistency. Immerse the eggs in cold water, then peel and slice into halves or quarters.

Peel the shallots and slice into fine rings. Toss the lamb's lettuce in some of the dressing, then arrange it in a bowl or on a shallow platter. Scatter the shallots, bacon, eggs, and crisps on top. Serve immediately with the remaining dressing alongside.

Tip: this recipe makes a generous amount of dressing so that everyone can help themselves to some extra. If any dressing is left over, you are all set for your next salad. Instead of bacon, try some smoked tofu for a vegetarian version.

This is a classic combination, which tastes fantastic as a salad.
Crunchy fennel and slightly sweet hints of aniseed from the dill
create an amazing flavour and help offset the acidity of the apple.

Danish herring and potato salad with apple and fennel

Serves 4–6
Preparation 20 minutes
Cook 25 minutes

For the salad
800g (1¾lb) waxy potatoes
salt and freshly ground
    black pepper
2 green apples
lemon juice
1 fennel bulb, with fronds
1 bunch of dill
200g (7oz) matjes
    (marinated herring fillet)
200ml (7fl oz) sour cream
150g (5½oz) full-fat
    natural yogurt
2 tbsp olive oil
1 pinch of granulated sugar

For the dressing
1 onion
olive oil for frying
100g (3½oz) bacon, cubed
250ml (9fl oz) vegetable
    stock
4 tbsp white wine vinegar

Peel the potatoes, then boil in lightly salted water for about 20–25 minutes until soft. Drain, leave to cool, dice, and transfer to a bowl.

To make the dressing, peel and dice the onion. Heat some oil in a frying pan and fry the onion and bacon over a moderate heat. Season with pepper, then add the stock and vinegar. Bring everything to the boil once more and then pour over the potatoes. Leave to cool.

Wash, halve, and core the apples. Slice into thin wedges and drizzle with lemon juice.

Wash the fennel and remove the base and any woody sections. Chop the fennel fronds. Slice the bulb very thinly using a knife or mandoline. Wash the dill, shake dry, and finely chop. Roughly chop the matjes. Add the apple wedges, fennel, dill, sour cream, yogurt, and oil to the potatoes. Mix everything thoroughly and season with salt, pepper, and sugar before serving.

Tip: this salad tastes great with buttered crispbreads.

Potatoes baked in the oven with strong spices work beautifully. Fresh vegetables ensure a fabulous firm texture, while the yogurt adds a creamy element and a welcome touch of acidity.

Baked potato salad with capers, artichokes, and yogurt

Vegetarian
Serves 4
Preparation 15 minutes
Cook 20 minutes

2 garlic cloves
freshly ground coarse
    sea salt
1 pinch of brown sugar
1 tsp ras-el-hanout
1 tsp hot paprika
juice and zest of ½
    organic lemon
5 tbsp olive oil
800g (1¾lb) small
    waxy potatoes
2 tbsp sesame seeds
2 red onions
1 red pointed pepper
1–2 tbsp capers
1 tin artichoke bottoms,
    about 150g (5½oz) drained
1 small piece of preserved
    lemon
250g (9oz) natural yogurt,
    stirred until creamy
5 sprigs of parsley
5 anchovy fillets (optional)
freshly ground black pepper

Preheat the oven to 180°C (160°C fan/350°F/Gas 4) and line a tray with baking paper. Peel and chop the garlic. Combine the garlic, salt, sugar, spices, lemon zest, juice, and oil in a bowl. Wash and halve the potatoes and add to the sesame seeds. Mix everything together well, spread over the lined tray, and bake in the oven for 20 minutes.

Meanwhile, peel the onions and slice into rings. Wash the pepper, slice in half, remove the seeds, and cut into strips. Roughly chop the capers. Slice the drained artichokes. Chop the preserved lemon and add to the yogurt. Wash the parsley and shake dry, then strip off the leaves.

Transfer the warm potatoes to a serving plate and arrange with the onions, pepper, capers, artichokes, and anchovies, if using. Drizzle with yogurt and sprinkle everything with salt, pepper, and parsley.

Tip: this salad also tastes great the following day – just readjust the seasoning with salt and pepper before serving.

CLASSIC RECIPES

Fried potatoes

Fried potatoes using raw potatoes

Serves 4
Preparation 10 minutes
Cook 15 minutes

800g (1¾lb) waxy potatoes
1 onion
150g (5½oz) streaky
   smoked bacon
olive oil or lard for frying
salt

Peel and dice the potatoes. Peel, halve, and slice the onion. Dice the bacon. Heat 1–2 tbsp oil or lard in a large non-stick frying pan. Fry all the chopped ingredients for 15 minutes, initially over a high heat, then over a moderate heat, tossing repeatedly and covering with a lid occasionally. As soon as the potatoes are cooked, season with salt and serve.

Tip: you can make these fried potatoes more interesting with some fresh or dried herbs, chopped garlic, or spices.

Fried potatoes using cooked potatoes

Vegan
Serves 4
Preparation 5 minutes
Cook 35 minutes

800g (1¾lb) waxy potatoes
sea salt
olive oil or lard for frying

Wash the potatoes and cook for 20–25 minutes in slightly salted water until soft. Drain and leave to cool completely. Peel and slice the potatoes. Heat 1–2 tbsp of oil or lard in a non-stick frying pan and fry the potatoes over a moderate heat, tossing frequently until crisp. Season with salt and serve immediately.

Tip: make this a more substantial dish by adding bacon and onions. First, fry the bacon and chopped onion until crisp, then add the sliced potatoes and continue frying until golden. Remember that less salt will be needed if you add bacon.

*This dish never gets dull – creamy mashed potatoes can be adapted
in all sorts of ways depending on the time of year and what you fancy.*

Mashed potatoes

Vegetarian
Serves 4
Preparation 10 minutes
Cook 25 minutes

1kg (2¼lb) floury potatoes
salt
180g (6oz) butter
1 pinch of grated nutmeg

Special equipment
hand-held blender

Peel the potatoes and boil in lightly salted water for 20–25 minutes until soft. Drain and retain the cooking water.
Add the butter in small pieces to the potatoes and mash them together with some of the cooking water. Season with salt and nutmeg.

To create a fine purée, roughly mash the potatoes and butter with a fork. Then use a hand-held blender to combine them with sufficient cooking liquid to create a creamy purée. Season to taste once you have the desired consistency.

For different options

Wasabi mash

2–4 tbsp wasabi (from a tube)

Flavour the mash with wasabi.

Lemon mash

1 organic lemon

Flavour the mash with some grated zest and juice from an organic lemon.

Beetroot mash

400g (14oz) cooked beetroots, vacuum packed

For the mashed potato, peel 600g (1lb 5oz) potatoes, cook as described, and mash with butter. Dice and purée the beetroots. Add the beetroot purée to the mashed potato and stir in some of the potato cooking water until you have a creamy consistency.

Tip: alternatively, you can use fresh beetroots. In which case, peel, grate, and cook them with the potatoes. Prepare the mash as described above.

Celeriac mash

1 celeriac bulb, about 400g (14oz)
1 pinch of dukkah or ras-el-hanout

Peel and dice the celeriac and cook it with 600g (1lb 5oz) potatoes. Follow the basic recipe to make the mash but season with dukkah or ras-el-hanout instead of nutmeg.

Pea mash

400g (14oz) frozen peas

Defrost the peas, purée, and add to the cooked potatoes. Prepare the mash as described previously.

Horseradish mash

½ jar horseradish sauce
grated horseradish root

Stir sufficient horseradish sauce and grated horseradish into the prepared mash to achieve the desired flavour. Sprinkle with grated horseradish before serving.

In Italian, the singular form of gnocchi is "gnocco", which translates as "dumpling". Bread dumplings are "gnocchi di pane" and yeast dumplings are "gnocchi di pasta lievitata". This recipe is for making traditional potato gnocchi.

Potato gnocchi

Vegetarian
Serves 4
Preparation 25 minutes
Cook 15 minutes

1kg (2¼lb) floury boiled
   potatoes (prepared
   previously)
2 small eggs
salt and freshly ground
   black pepper
100g (3½oz) flour, plus extra
   for working
olive oil for drizzling
butter for frying
sage or herbs of your choice

Special equipment
potato ricer

Peel the cooked potatoes and mash them in a bowl using a potato ricer. Make a hole in the centre and crack the eggs into it. Sprinkle the salt and flour around the eggs. Quickly knead everything together to create a smooth and elastic dough and shape this into a ball. If it is too sticky, add a little more flour.

Divide the dough into four pieces and roll each one out on the floured work surface to create long strands of the same thickness. Chop these into 2–2.5cm- (³/₄–1in-) wide pieces and use a fork to mould each one into the traditional gnocchi shape. Do not leave the gnocchi to stand too long or they may go soft and lose their shape.

Bring about 2 litres (3¹/₂ pints) lightly salted water to the boil in a large saucepan and add half the gnocchi, then lower the heat. The gnocchi should cook at just below boiling point until they all float to the surface. Use a slotted spoon to scoop the gnocchi out of the water. Transfer to a tray or shallow plate and drizzle with oil. Cook the remaining gnocchi in the same way.

Before serving, fry the gnocchi in butter with a few sage leaves or herbs of your choice and season with salt and pepper.

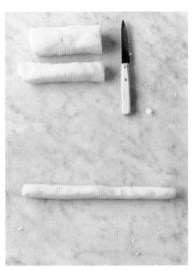
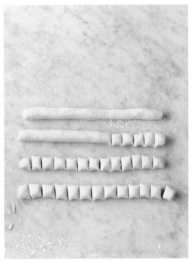
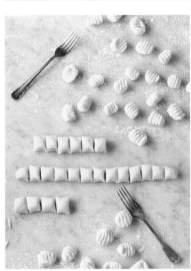

Tip: cooked, cooled gnocchi can be kept in the fridge until you are ready to use them. They can also be frozen. Try adding some herbs to the potato dough if you like. Just add the chopped herbs to the dough mixture before kneading it to a smooth consistency.

Home-made fries and potato wedges

French fries

Vegan
Serves 4
Preparation 10 minutes
Cook 20 minutes

1kg (2¼lb) large
    floury potatoes
about 2 litres (3½ pints)
    vegetable oil or fat for
    deep frying
salt

Peel the potatoes and slice into 5mm- (¼in-) thick chip shapes. Heat the oil to 160°C (320°F) in a high-sided pan and pre-cook the potatoes in batches for 2–3 minutes. Leave them to drain on kitchen towel.

Increase the temperature of the oil to 180°C (355°F) and fry the chips again for about

4–6 minutes until golden brown. Drain the chips thoroughly, transfer to a bowl, season with salt, and serve immediately.

Tip: it is essential to double fry the potatoes to create crisp chips. If you don't want to fry them twice in oil, you can use a hot air fryer for the first frying stage.

Potato wedges

Vegan
Serves 4
Preparation 10 minutes
Cook 40 minutes

1kg (2¼lb) medium
    waxy potatoes
4 tbsp neutral-tasting
    vegetable oil
ground sea salt
ground paprika or chilli
    flakes and spices
    (optional)
50g (1¾oz) polenta

Preheat the oven to 200°C (180°C fan/400°F/Gas 6). Wash the potatoes and slice them evenly into wedges.

Combine the oil, salt, your preferred spices, if using, and polenta in a large bowl. Add the potato wedges and mix everything together well.

Line two baking trays with baking paper, spread the wedges on top, and bake for 30–40 minutes until crisp.

Two things are essential to achieve chips that are crisp on the outside and beautifully creamy on the inside: a floury variety of potato and a double-frying process.

Traditional rösti

Rösti made from cooked potatoes

Vegetarian
Serves 4 as a side dish
Preparation 10 minutes
Cook 20 minutes

800g (1¾lb) waxy boiled
  potatoes (prepared
  previously)
salt
1 pinch of grated nutmeg
3 tbsp oil or clarified butter
  for frying

Peel and grate the potatoes and
season with salt and nutmeg.
Heat 2 tbsp oil or clarified butter
in a non-stick 24cm- (9¹/₂in-)
diameter frying pan and add the
potato mixture. Use a spatula to
press down slightly along the
sides of the mixture to give it a
firm edge. Fry the rösti over a
moderate heat for 6–8 minutes,

then slide it onto a plate and use
a second plate on top to turn it
over. Add the remaining 1 tbsp
oil or clarified butter to the pan
and slide the rösti back into the
pan with the uncooked side
facing down. Cook the rösti until
the second side is golden and
serve immediately.

Rösti made from raw potatoes

Serves 4 as a side dish
Preparation 10 minutes
Cook 25 minutes

1 onion
75g (2½oz) streaky
  smoked bacon
700g (1lb 9oz) waxy potatoes
salt
1 pinch of grated nutmeg
3 tbsp oil or lard for frying

Peel and finely dice the onion.
Dice the bacon. Peel and grate
the potatoes and season with
salt and nutmeg. Heat 2 tbsp
oil or lard in a non-stick 24cm-
(9¹/₂in-) diameter frying pan.
Add the bacon and onion and
fry over a moderate heat. Add
the potatoes and use a spatula
to press down slightly along the
sides of the mixture to give it a

firm edge. Fry the rösti for
8–10 minutes, then slide it onto
a plate and use a second plate
on top to turn it over. Add the
remaining 1 tbsp oil or lard to
the pan and slide the rösti back
into the pan with the uncooked
side facing down. Cook the rösti
until the second side is golden
and serve immediately.

Rösti is a classic German and Swiss dish, but nobody can agree whether the original was made using raw or cooked potatoes. Why not try out both options and decide for yourself which you prefer? Just serve a small salad and a fried egg with your rösti for a complete main course.

Potato cakes or fritters are popular all over the world in different variations.
Also known as potato pancakes, they can be served with a savoury or sweet
accompaniment. This version is delicious served with apple sauce.

Potato cakes or fritters

Vegetarian
Serves 4
Preparation 15 minutes
Cook 15 minutes

1kg (2¼lb) waxy potatoes
1 onion
2 eggs
1 tbsp potato starch
salt
1 pinch of grated nutmeg
4 tbsp vegetable oil or
    clarified butter for frying
apple sauce to serve

Peel and finely grate the potatoes. Use kitchen towel to squeeze out as much liquid as possible in batches. Peel and finely chop the onion. Combine the onion, potatoes, eggs, and potato starch in a bowl, and season with salt and nutmeg.

Heat the oil or clarified butter in a non-stick frying pan. Use two spoons or damp hands to shape the mixture into fritters, then fry them in the hot fat on both sides until golden. Drain on kitchen towel and serve with apple sauce.

Tip: add some herbs, chopped garlic, or spices to make the potato fritters even more delicious. A grated carrot or courgette also works well in the mixture.

Potato dumplings are popular in many parts of Europe, particularly Germany and Austria. They can be made from cooked potato or a combination of cooked and uncooked potatoes.

Potato dumplings

Vegetarian
Makes 20 dumplings,
  serves 4

Tip for both varieties: before serving, pour some melted butter or breadcrumbs toasted in butter over the dumplings and scatter with chopped parsley. What you serve them with makes these dumplings interesting. Possible options include toasted croutons with sea salt and garlic, or fried bacon and onions. The combinations are limitless.

Using up leftovers: if you have dumplings left over from the previous day, you can slice and pan fry them. Children absolutely love these! Fry slices of dumpling with some onion and mushrooms for a really delicious treat.

Dumplings made from cooked potatoes

Preparation 10 minutes
Cook 40 minutes

800g (1¾lb) floury potatoes
salt
1 pinch of grated nutmeg
75g (2½oz) plain flour
75g (2½oz) potato starch
1 egg

Special equipment
potato ricer

Wash the potatoes, then boil in lightly salted water for about 25–30 minutes until soft. Drain and let the potatoes steam thoroughly in the saucepan. Peel and mash the potatoes using a potato ricer while they are still hot. Leave to cool.

Season the potatoes with salt and nutmeg. Add the flour, starch, and egg, then knead everything swiftly to create a smooth dough. With lightly floured hands, shape about 50g ($1^3/_4$oz) of this mixture to make each dumpling.

Bring a large pan of slightly salted water to the boil, add the dumplings in batches, and cook at just below boiling point until they float to the surface. Remove with a slotted spoon and serve immediately.

Half-and-half dumplings made from raw and cooked potatoes

Preparation 15 minutes
Cook 40 minutes

800g (1¾lb) floury potatoes
salt
1 pinch of grated nutmeg
80g (2¾oz) potato starch
1 egg

Special equipment
potato ricer

Peel the potatoes and boil half of them (400g/14oz) in lightly salted water for about 25–30 minutes until soft. Drain and let the potatoes steam thoroughly in the saucepan. Mash the potatoes using a potato ricer while they are still hot.

Finely grate the remaining potatoes and thoroughly squeeze out any liquid in a sieve or with a piece of muslin. Combine the raw and cooked potatoes in a bowl and season with salt and nutmeg. Add the potato starch and egg, and knead everything swiftly to create a smooth dough. Shape about 50g (1³/₄oz) of this mixture to make each dumpling.

Bring a large pan of slightly salted water to the boil, add the dumplings in batches, and cook at just below boiling point until they float to the surface. Remove with a slotted spoon and serve immediately.

"Schupfis", or potato noodles, are a local delicacy in southern German and Austrian cuisine. They are also often referred to as "finger noodles", no doubt due to their shape.

Schupfnudeln

Vegetarian
Serves 4
Preparation 15 minutes
Cook 15 minutes

1kg (2¼lb) boiled floury
    potatoes (prepared
    previously)
1 egg
2–3 egg yolks
salt
200g (7oz) plain flour, plus
    extra for working
melted butter to serve

Special equipment
potato ricer

Peel the cooked potatoes and mash them in a bowl using a potato ricer. Make a hole in the centre and crack the egg and egg yolks into this. Sprinkle the salt and flour around the eggs, and quickly knead everything to create a smooth and elastic dough. Shape the dough into a ball, adding a little more flour if it is too sticky.

Divide the dough into four pieces, and roll each one out on a floured work surface to create strands that are about as thick as your finger. Divide these strands into 5cm- (2in-) long pieces and roll them to make potato noodles with tapered ends.

Bring about 2 litres (3¹/₂ pints) lightly salted water to the boil in a large saucepan and add the noodles in two batches. Lower

the heat – they should cook at just below boiling point until they float to the surface. Remove the noodles from the pan with a slotted spoon.

As soon as all the noodles are cooked, drizzle them with melted butter and serve.

Tip: traditionally, potato noodles are served with sauerkraut, but they make a great side dish for almost any recipe. Another option is to put the potato noodles on a tray or plate, drizzle with olive oil, then fry in butter before serving, seasoning to taste with salt and nutmeg. You can also fry them with onions and mushrooms and serve with a salad for a delicious main course.

Hasselback potatoes are a Swedish speciality. They were invented in the 1950s by chef Leif Elisson at the Hasselbacken restaurant in Stockholm.

Hasselback potatoes

Vegetarian
Serves 4
Preparation 15 minutes
Cook 45 minutes

3 garlic cloves
4 sprigs of herbs of your
    choice (e.g. rosemary,
    thyme, sage)
100g (3½oz) butter
1kg (2¼lb) medium waxy
    potatoes
freshly ground coarse
    sea salt

Preheat the oven to 220°C (200°C fan/425°F/Gas 7). Line a baking tray with baking paper. Peel and chop the garlic. Wash the herbs and shake dry, strip the leaves, and chop. Melt the butter in a saucepan.

Wash the potatoes thoroughly and slice them part of the way through with a sharp knife. Make sure you do not slice them all the way through – place each potato between two wooden skewers to help with cutting.

Place the potatoes on the baking tray and sprinkle with garlic, herbs, and sea salt so that the

seasoning goes in between the slices of potato. Pour the melted butter over the potatoes and bake for 45 minutes in the oven. If they are turning too dark, cover the potatoes with aluminium foil after 30 minutes. Serve immediately.

Tip: Hasselback potatoes taste fabulous with meat that has been briefly seared or some fish. Serve with a salad and a dip for a vegetarian main course.

Croquettes are found all over Europe in various forms and with different fillings. These potato croquettes are a classic side dish served in French cuisine.

Croquettes

Vegetarian
Serves 4
Preparation 20 minutes
Cook 45 minutes

1kg (2¼lb) floury potatoes
salt
5 small eggs
1 pinch of grated nutmeg
150g (5½oz) plain flour
250g (9oz) breadcrumbs
1 litre (1¾ pints) neutral-
    tasting vegetable oil
    suitable for deep frying

Special equipment
potato ricer
piping bag

Peel the potatoes, then boil in lightly salted water for about 25–30 minutes until soft. Drain and leave the potatoes to steam on the hob with the heat turned off. Stir the potatoes occasionally during this process to make sure they are completely dry as otherwise the croquettes will fall apart when you fry them.

Separate four of the eggs. Mash the potatoes using a potato ricer, season with salt and nutmeg, and stir in the egg yolks. Transfer the mixture to a piping bag without a nozzle, and pipe shapes about the width of your thumb and 4cm (1¹/₂in) long on a floured work surface.

Whisk the remaining egg with the egg whites and a pinch of salt to use for coating the croquettes with breadcrumbs. Put the flour and breadcrumbs into two separate bowls. First, toss the croquettes in the flour, then dip them in the egg, and finally coat them in the breadcrumbs.

Preheat the oven to 140°C (120°C fan/275°F/Gas 1). Line a baking tray with kitchen towel. Heat the oil to 160–180°C (320–355°F) in a large frying pan. Add the croquettes in batches and fry until golden. Remove with a slotted spoon, transfer to the lined tray, and keep warm in the oven. Once you have fried all the croquettes, serve immediately.

Tip: instead of frying the croquettes in oil, you can also bake them in the oven. Place the uncooked croquettes on a tray lined with baking paper and bake in a preheated oven at 220°C (200°C fan/425°F/Gas 7) for 20 minutes. Turn the croquettes occasionally while cooking.

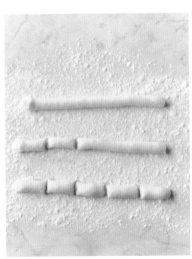

Croquettes with cheese, herbs, and pine nuts

Preparation 30 minutes
Cook 45 minutes

30g (1oz) pine nuts
4 sprigs of parsley
4 sprigs of basil
1 garlic clove
70g (2¼oz) grated Parmesan
  or pecorino
salt and freshly ground
  black pepper

Toast the pine nuts in a dry pan and chop finely. Wash the herbs, shake dry, strip the leaves, and chop. Peel and chop the garlic. Stir the pine nuts, herbs, garlic, and grated cheese into the potato mixture, season with salt and pepper, and continue cooking as described opposite.

Tip: instead of long croquettes, you can also make round balls.

*This is a basic recipe that is a popular side dish with simple home-cooked food.
It can be a bit too rich served this way, so a good option is to serve it with a
fresh salad as a simple lunch or supper.*

Classic potato gratin

Vegetarian
Serves 4
Preparation 20 minutes
Cook 50 minutes

butter for greasing
1kg (2¼lb) waxy potatoes
2 garlic cloves
salt
125ml (4fl oz) single cream
200ml (7fl oz) milk
1 pinch of grated nutmeg
150g (5½oz) grated Gruyère

Preheat the oven to 220°C
(200°C fan/425°F/Gas 7).
Grease a 20 x 30cm (8 x 12in)
ovenproof dish with butter. Peel
the potatoes and slice very thinly
using a knife or mandoline. When
slicing, try to hold the potatoes
together so you can pack them
as tightly as possible in the dish.

Peel and chop the garlic and
crush it to a paste with some
salt. Combine the garlic paste,
cream, milk, and nutmeg. Pour
this mixture over the potatoes.
Cover the dish with aluminium
foil and bake the gratin in the
oven for 40 minutes.

Remove the gratin from the oven
and increase the temperature
to 240°C (220°C fan/475°F/
Gas 9). Remove the foil, scatter
the grated cheese over the
gratin, and return to the oven for
10 minutes until golden brown.

Tip: for a cauliflower and potato
gratin, simply blanch some
cauliflower briefly and add this
in layers between the potato.
This gratin also tastes great with
Brussels sprouts and bacon.

MAIN COURSES

This goulash is meat-free, spicy, and a great basic recipe with lots of potential variations. Try flavouring it with herbes de Provence and garlic, or some spices such as za'atar, ras-el-hanout, or cumin.

Spicy potato goulash

Vegetarian
Serves 4
Preparation 15 minutes
Cook 35 minutes

1kg (2¼lb) waxy potatoes
2 onions
3 garlic cloves
200g (7oz) celery
olive oil for frying
2 tbsp tomato purée
salt
1 tsp ground paprika
1 tsp cayenne pepper
1 tsp harissa powder
500ml (16fl oz) vegetable
  stock
a few sprigs of marjoram
a few sprigs of thyme
500g (1lb 2oz) cherry
  tomatoes
½ bunch of parsley
½ bunch of chives
100ml (3½fl oz) sour cream

Peel and roughly dice the potatoes. Peel and finely dice the onions and garlic. Wash the celery and cut into strips.

Heat some oil in a large frying pan. Sauté the potatoes and celery, stirring constantly. Lower the heat and add the onions, garlic, and tomato purée. Next, stir in the salt, paprika, cayenne pepper, and harissa powder, followed by the stock. Wash the marjoram and thyme and shake dry, then add both to the pan.

Bring the goulash to the boil, cover, and simmer over a low heat for 30 minutes. Add more stock if necessary. During the final 10 minutes of the cooking

time, remove the lid, add the tomatoes, and continue cooking the goulash down to a thick consistency.

Meanwhile, wash the parsley and chives and shake dry. Strip the parsley leaves from the stalks and chop them finely with the chives. Season the goulash to taste with salt, paprika, and cayenne pepper, then serve with the chopped herbs and sour cream.

Tip: if you like, you can fry 500g (1lb 2oz) minced meat or 200g (7oz) diced streaky bacon with the vegetables. Smoked tofu makes another great addition to this goulash.

Cottage pie is traditionally made with tender beef mince covered with a layer of creamy potatoes, but it's also excellent with a mixture of different types of minced meat.

Cottage pie

Makes 1 pie, 26cm (10¼in) diameter
Preparation 15 minutes
Cook 1 hour 10 minutes

800g (1¾lb) floury potatoes
salt and freshly ground
    black pepper
1 large onion
2 garlic cloves
2 carrots
4 sticks celery
a few sprigs of rosemary,
    thyme, and sage, or dried
    herbes de Provence
olive oil for frying
600g (1lb 5oz) minced meat,
    half beef, half pork
400g can chopped tomatoes
1 tbsp tomato purée
1 pinch of granulated sugar
200ml (7fl oz) milk
1 pinch of grated nutmeg
butter for greasing
100g (3½oz) grated hard
    cheese (e.g. Cheddar
    or Parmesan)

Preheat the oven to 200°C (180°C fan/400°F/Gas 6). Peel the potatoes, then boil in lightly salted water for about 20–25 minutes until soft. Meanwhile, peel and finely chop the onion and garlic. Clean the carrots and celery and finely dice them. Wash the herbs, shake dry, strip the leaves from the stalks, and chop.

Heat some oil in a large frying pan and sauté the mince. Add the vegetables and herbs and continue cooking, stirring frequently. Add the tomatoes with their juice and the tomato purée, and simmer everything until the liquid has boiled off. Season with salt, pepper, and sugar.

Drain the potatoes thoroughly, then mash. Heat the milk, stir it into the mash, and season with salt, pepper, and nutmeg. Grease a pie dish or casserole with butter. Transfer the cooked meat into the dish, spread the mash over the top, and sprinkle with grated cheese. Bake in the oven for 45 minutes until the top is golden brown.

Tip: if you have leftovers from your roast or some uneaten meatballs to use up, they taste fantastic in this pie. You can make a vegetarian option using tofu and a variety of mushrooms.

The crunchy crust made from Parmesan and fried onions adds an element of surprise to this casserole, which is based on a recipe Granny used to make. It is essentially a cross between a gratin and a stew, if you can imagine such a thing.

Granny's hearty Savoy cabbage, mince, and potato casserole

Serves 4–6
Preparation 15 minutes
Cook 1 hour 20 minutes

1kg (2¼lb) waxy potatoes
salt and freshly ground
    black pepper
½ Savoy cabbage
2 onions
3 garlic cloves
1 chilli (optional)
200g (7oz) streaky bacon
oil for frying
500g (1lb 2oz) minced meat,
    half beef, half pork
1 pinch of grated nutmeg
1 pinch of ground paprika
1 pinch of granulated sugar
1 tbsp lemon juice
butter for greasing
2 eggs
100g (3½oz) grated Parmesan
4 handfuls of fried onions

Peel the potatoes, then boil in lightly salted water for about 20–25 minutes until soft. Drain and cut into medium cubes.

Remove the stalk from the Savoy cabbage, then wash the leaves and shake dry before slicing them into strips. Bring plenty of salted water to the boil in a saucepan and blanch the Savoy cabbage briefly, making sure it remains crisp. Remove the cabbage with a slotted spoon and reserve the cooking liquid.

Peel and dice the onions and garlic. If using, wash the chilli, slice in half lengthways, remove the seeds, and chop finely. Dice the bacon. Heat some oil in a large frying pan over a high heat and briskly sauté the bacon and mince. Lower the heat slightly and add the onions, garlic, and chilli, if using. Season with salt, pepper, nutmeg, ground paprika, sugar, and lemon juice.

Preheat the oven to 180°C (160°C fan/350°F/Gas 4). Grease a deep 30 × 40cm (12 x 16in) ovenproof dish with butter. Layer the potatoes, meat, and Savoy cabbage in any order. Whisk the eggs with 500ml (16fl oz) reserved water from blanching the cabbage. Pour this over the casserole and cook in the centre of the oven for 35–40 minutes.

Scatter the grated cheese and fried onions over the dish, increase the oven temperature to 220°C (200°C fan/425°F/Gas 7), and continue cooking for 10–15 minutes until golden brown on top.

Tip: if you happen to have leftovers, you can easily reheat this dish, and it tastes just as good the second time round.

Potatoes are ideal for vegan cooking: they contain lots of vitamins, minerals, and high-quality protein. Here, cashews are added for extra protein and B vitamins.

Vegan potato and spinach gratin with crispy sesame seeds

Vegan
Serves 4
Preparation 30 minutes
Cook 50 minutes

For the gratin
150g (5½oz) cashews
200ml (7fl oz) vegetable
    stock
olive oil for greasing
800g (1¾lb) waxy potatoes
1 onion
2 garlic cloves
1 piece of ginger, about
    3cm (1¼in)
350g (12oz) frozen spinach,
    defrosted
2 tsp coriander seeds
1 tsp cumin
salt

For the sesame seeds
50g (1¾oz) coarse
    breadcrumbs
2 tbsp sesame seeds
2 tsp ras-el-hanout
4 tbsp olive oil

Special equipment
hand-held blender

Add the cashews and stock to a bowl and set aside for 30 minutes. Then use a hand-held blender to purée to a fine consistency.

Grease a 25 × 30cm (10 x 12in) or 24cm (9¹/₂in) round ovenproof dish with oil and preheat the oven to 180°C (160°C fan/350°F/Gas 4). Peel and slice the potatoes very thinly. Spread half the potatoes in the dish and cover with half of the cashew cream.

Peel and finely dice the onion, garlic, and ginger. In a bowl, combine the spinach, onion, garlic, ginger, spices, and ½ tsp salt. Spread this mixture over the

potatoes, then top with the remaining potatoes. Pour in the rest of the cashew cream, shaking the dish slightly to distribute everything evenly.

Bake the gratin in the oven for 30 minutes. To make the sesame seed topping, combine the breadcrumbs, sesame seeds, ras-el-hanout, and oil. Remove the gratin from the oven, sprinkle over the sesame mixture and continue cooking for 15–20 minutes.

Tip: to make the breadcrumbs, just dice a stale piece of rye bread and blitz it in a food processor.

Smashed potatoes

Serves 4
Preparation 10 minutes
Cook 50 minutes

1kg (2¼lb) small
   waxy potatoes
salt
1 garlic clove
5 tbsp olive oil
2 tsp dried herbs
1 tsp sweet ground paprika
coarse sea salt

Wash the potatoes and boil in lightly salted water for 15–20 minutes until soft. Just before the end of the cooking time, preheat the oven to 220°C (200°C fan/ 425°F/Gas 7) and line a baking tray with baking paper.

Drain the potatoes, spread them over the tray, and press down on them with the base of a saucepan so they are about 1.5cm (⅝in) thick. Peel and chop the garlic. Combine the garlic, olive oil, herbs, and ground paprika. Brush the potatoes with this mixture, sprinkle with coarse sea salt, and bake in the oven for 30 minutes.

Try one of the following suggestions for added variety.

Salmon with a honey and mustard sauce

3 tbsp honey
2 tbsp medium-hot mustard
1 tbsp wholegrain mustard
3 sprigs of dill
salt and freshly ground
   black pepper
150g (5½oz) smoked salmon

Combine the honey with both types of mustard. Wash the dill, remove the stalks, and chop finely. Stir the dill into the honey and mustard mixture and season with salt and pepper.

Serve the potatoes with salmon and the mustard sauce.

Radishes, ginger and coriander dip, and mint yogurt

Vegetarian

6 sprigs of fresh mint
300g (10oz) Greek yogurt
1 tsp ground turmeric
salt and freshly ground
   black pepper
1 piece ginger, about
   2cm (¾in)
1 tsp coriander seeds
2 tsp honey
2 tbsp balsamic vinegar
2 tbsp olive oil
1 bunch of radishes

Wash the mint, dab dry, strip the leaves, and chop. Combine the yogurt, mint, and turmeric, and season with salt and pepper. Use a spoon to scrape the skin off the ginger, then grate finely. Grind the coriander seeds with a pestle and mortar.

Combine the coriander, ginger, honey, vinegar, and oil, and season with salt and pepper.

Wash the radishes and slice thinly. Serve the potatoes and radishes with the ginger and coriander dip and mint yogurt.

This recipe for smashed potatoes makes a great side dish, but it can also be turned into a quick main course with some suitable dips.

Subtle bitter notes are combined with a hint of sweetness and savoury cheese in this baked dish. The potatoes and cream create a smooth foundation.

Potato and chicory bake with raisins and blue cheese

Vegetarian
Serves 4
Preparation 15 minutes
Cook 35 minutes

800g (1¾lb) waxy potatoes
salt and freshly ground
  black pepper
3 chicory bulbs
1 tbsp butter
3 tbsp raisins
100ml (3½fl oz) white port
150g (5½oz) blue cheese
150ml (5fl oz) whipping
  cream
2–3 pinches of grated
  nutmeg
2 sprigs of rosemary

Peel and dice the potatoes. Boil in lightly salted water for 10 minutes. Meanwhile, wash the chicory and slice into 2cm (³/₄in) chunks. Melt the butter in a frying pan over a moderate heat and sauté the chicory. Add the raisins and season with salt and pepper. Pour in the port and simmer to reduce the liquid.

Drain the potatoes and leave them briefly to steam. Dice the cheese. Combine the potatoes, cheese, and chicory and transfer into a single large casserole dish or several individual ovenproof dishes.

Preheat the oven to 200°C (180°C fan/400°F/Gas 6). Season the cream with a small amount of salt, 2–3 pinches of nutmeg, and pepper, then pour this over the vegetables. Wash the rosemary and dab dry, strip the leaves from the stalks, and scatter over the casserole. Bake in the oven for 20–25 minutes until golden brown all over. Serve hot.

Tip: if you prefer, you can purée the cheese with the seasoned cream then pour this over the vegetables.

Children love this creamy potato lasagne, and thanks to the potatoes, cashews, and tofu, it contains lots of protein and valuable vitamins.

Vegan potato and cashew lasagne with sautéed leeks

Vegan
Serves 4
Preparation 15 minutes
Cook 1 hour

100g (3½oz) cashews
3 leeks
2 tbsp olive oil, plus extra
    for greasing
salt and freshly ground
    black pepper
1 pinch of grated nutmeg
150g (5½oz) smoked tofu
2 tsp yeast flakes
1 onion
2 garlic cloves
2 sprigs of rosemary
2 sprigs of thyme
3 tbsp tomato purée
400g can chopped tomatoes
6 large waxy potatoes

Special equipment
hand-held blender

Soak the cashews in lukewarm water for 10 minutes. Trim, wash, and slice the leeks. Heat the oil in a frying pan, sauté the leeks, and season with salt and nutmeg. Crumble in the tofu and mix this into the leeks. Drain the soaked cashews and use a hand-held blender to purée finely with 150ml (5fl oz) fresh water and the yeast flakes.

Peel and dice the onion and garlic. Wash the rosemary and thyme, shake dry, strip the leaves from the stalks, and chop. Combine the tomato purée, chopped tomatoes with their juice, herbs, onion, and garlic, and season with salt and pepper. Peel the potatoes, then slice thinly lengthways.

Preheat the oven to 200°C (180°C fan/400°F/Gas 6). Grease an ovenproof dish with oil, line with the slices from two potatoes, and cover with one-third of the cashew cream. Top with half the leek and tofu mixture and half the tomato sauce. Repeat the layers of potatoes, cashew cream, leek and tofu mixture, and tomato sauce. Top with the remaining slices of potato and some cashew cream. Bake the lasagne in the oven for 50–60 minutes and serve hot.

Tip: you can top it with grated Emmental, Gruyère, or pecorino for a non-vegan lasagne.

A summer vegetable traybake that also tastes great cold, this is the perfect side dish for a barbecue.

Oven-roasted potatoes, Swiss chard, and feta

Vegetarian
Serves 4
Preparation 15 minutes
Cook 45 minutes

3 garlic cloves
½ bunch of thyme
750g (1lb 10oz) waxy
  potatoes
5 tbsp olive oil
sea salt
800g (1¾lb) Swiss chard
juice of ½ lemon
1 tsp honey
1 pinch of cayenne pepper
200g (7oz) feta

Preheat the oven to 220°C (200°C fan/425°F/Gas 7). Line a baking tray with baking paper. Peel the garlic cloves and slice in half. Wash the thyme, shake dry, and strip off the leaves. Peel the potatoes, slice into bitesize pieces, and spread over the tray. Drizzle with 3 tbsp oil, sprinkle over 1 tsp sea salt, the garlic and thyme, and mix well. Bake in the centre of the oven for 30 minutes.

Trim and wash the Swiss chard. Chop the leaves and stalks into bitesize pieces. Combine the remaining 2 tbsp oil, 2–3 pinches of salt, lemon juice, honey, and cayenne pepper in a bowl. Add the Swiss chard and toss in the marinade. Crumble or dice the feta.

Lower the oven temperature to 200°C (180°C fan/400°F/Gas 6). Turn the potatoes, scatter the Swiss chard and its marinade over the top followed by the feta, and continue baking for 15 minutes.

Tip: this dish tastes fabulous with some flatbread and hummus. The chickpea and vegetarian dips on p145 also make great accompaniments.

Home-made curry paste gives this potato curry a particularly aromatic flavour, allowing the toasted and freshly ground spices to unfold their complex aromas perfectly.

Malaysian potato curry with pineapple and peanuts

Vegan
Serves 4
Preparation 20 minutes
Cook 25 minutes

3 shallots
2 garlic cloves
1 piece of ginger, about
    3cm (1¼in)
1 green chilli
1 lemongrass stalk
100ml (3½fl oz) vegetable
    stock
2 star anise
4 cloves
3 green cardamom pods,
    seeds only
1 cinnamon stick
2 tsp coriander seeds
750g (1lb 10oz)
    waxy potatoes
2 tbsp groundnut oil
200ml (7fl oz) coconut milk
salt and freshly ground
    black pepper
50g (1¾oz) peanuts
½ pineapple
1 bunch of coriander
2–3 tbsp coconut flakes
lime wedges (optional)

Special equipment
hand-held blender

Peel the shallots and garlic. Use a spoon to scrape the skin off the ginger. Wash and deseed the chilli. Roughly chop all these ingredients. Wash the lemongrass and slice very thinly. Use a hand-held blender to finely purée these chopped ingredients with the vegetable stock to make a curry paste.

Toast the spices in a dry pan, leave to cool, then grind using a pestle and mortar. Peel the potatoes and chop into bitesize pieces. Heat the oil in a wok or deep pan over a high heat and briskly fry the potatoes for 5 minutes until they have browned. Add the curry paste, ground spices, and coconut milk. Season the curry with salt and pepper, cover, and simmer for 20 minutes.

Meanwhile, chop the peanuts and toast them in a dry pan. Peel the pineapple, remove the leaves, and chop into cubes. Add the pineapple to the curry and allow it warm through for 2–3 minutes. Wash the coriander, dab dry, and roughly shred.

Decant the curry into bowls and garnish with peanuts, coriander, and coconut flakes. Serve with lime wedges, if using.

Tip: for a quicker version of this recipe, just use a ready-made curry paste. Make sure you buy a good-quality product.

Salted potatoes and beetroot with dips

Serves 4
Preparation 5 minutes
Cook 1½ hours

8 medium beetroots
8 medium waxy potatoes
2kg (4½lb) coarse sea salt
2 tbsp olive oil

Preheat the oven to 180°C (160°C fan/350°F/Gas 4). Carefully wash the beetroots and potatoes. If there are stalks on the beetroots, trim them to 2cm (³/₄in). Spread half the salt over a baking tray. Rub the oil into the beetroots and potatoes,

place them on the salt, and cover with the remaining salt. Bake for 1 hour 30 minutes.

Remove the potatoes and beetroots from the salt, peel, and serve with the following dips.

144

These dips are ideal to make in advance and it's very easy to cook the vegetables in salt. In other words this is fun, healthy, "fast food".

Chickpea and curry dip

Vegan
1 garlic clove
1 can chickpeas, 200g (7oz), drained
1 pinch of chilli flakes
1 tsp ground cumin
2 tsp curry powder
about 100ml (3½fl oz) vegetable stock)

juice of ½ lemon
salt and freshly ground black pepper
drizzle of olive oil, to serve

Special equipment
blender

Peel the garlic and add to a blender beaker with the chickpeas, spices, stock, and lemon juice. Purée until smooth. Season the dip with salt and pepper, transfer to a small bowl, and drizzle with oil.

Trout dip

2 smoked trout fillets
100ml (3½fl oz) sour cream
100g (3½oz) full-fat cream cheese
juice of ½ lemon
salt

cayenne pepper
3–4 tbsp cress or microgreens of your choice

Special equipment
blender

Shred the trout fillets into small pieces. Purée the fish, sour cream, cream cheese, and lemon juice in a blender, and season with salt and cayenne pepper. Transfer to a small bowl and scatter with cress or microgreens.

Herby dip

Vegetarian
4 sprigs of flat-leaf parsley
4 sprigs of fresh coriander
½ bunch of chives
3 sprigs of dill
150g (5½oz) fat-free quark
75ml (2½fl oz) full-fat crème fraîche

1 tsp cider vinegar
1 tsp honey
salt and freshly ground black pepper

Wash the herbs and dab dry. Discard the stalks from the parsley, coriander, and dill, then chop these with the chives. Combine the herbs, quark, crème fraîche, vinegar, and honey, then season with salt and pepper and transfer to a small bowl.

Strictly speaking, this Spanish omelette is called tortilla de patatas to distinguish it from the French version, tortilla francesca, which does not contain potatoes. The word "tortilla" can also refer to the corn flatbreads from Mexico.

Tortilla with chorizo, roasted peppers, and Manchego

Serves 4
Preparation 10 minutes
Cook 25 minutes

3 waxy potatoes
salt and freshly ground
  black pepper
1 onion
1 garlic clove
5 sprigs of thyme
2 roasted peppers, drained
100g (3½oz) chorizo
8 eggs
2 tbsp olive oil
75g (2½oz) grated Manchego
2 tbsp cress or microgreens
  (varieties with different-
  coloured leaves are
  particularly good, such
  as beetroot, broccoli, or
  fenugreek microgreens)

Peel and slice the potatoes, boil for 10 minutes in lightly salted water, then drain. Peel and dice the onion and garlic. Wash the thyme and dab dry. Strip the leaves from the stalks. Chop the peppers. Peel and slice the chorizo. Whisk the eggs in a bowl with ½ tsp salt and a pinch of pepper.

Preheat the oven to 180°C (160°C fan/350°F/Gas 4). Heat the oil in an ovenproof pan and sauté the onion, garlic, and thyme. Add the chorizo and continue cooking. Add the potatoes and peppers, then pour in the eggs.

Scatter the grated Manchego over the tortilla and bake in the oven for 10–15 minutes until done. Slice the tortilla into portions and serve scattered with cress or microgreens.

Tip: this tortilla is an ideal way to use up leftover potatoes, and you can also vary the other ingredients to suit. In spring you could try using asparagus and peas or perhaps a hearty beetroot and rocket version.

The traditional Tyrolean gröstl recipe is designed to use up roast leftovers, including the potatoes. It is often served with a fried egg on top and any gravy left from the roast. This is a vegan version, which contains squash and chanterelle mushrooms in addition to potatoes for a colourful and nutritious meal that is packed with flavour.

Vegan gröstl with tofu, squash, and chanterelles

Vegan
Serves 4
Preparation 10 minutes
Cook 15 minutes

6 waxy boiled potatoes
   (prepared previously)
½ Hokkaido squash
200g (7oz) chanterelles
1 red onion
3–4 tbsp olive oil
150g (5½oz) smoked tofu
salt and freshly ground
   black pepper
1 tsp caraway seed
1 tsp sweet ground paprika
1 bunch of chives

Peel and slice the potatoes. Wash the squash, remove the seeds and any fibres, then dice. Clean the chanterelles and rub dry with kitchen towel, removing any pieces of soil. Peel and dice the onion.

Heat the oil in a frying pan over a moderate to high heat. Sauté the potatoes and squash until brown, turning constantly. Add the onion and chanterelles and continue frying for 2–3 minutes. Crumble the tofu into the pan, heat briefly, then season everything with salt, pepper, caraway seeds, and paprika. Wash the chives, dab dry, chop, and scatter over the gröstl.

Tip: pesto tastes delicious with gröstl for a non-vegan version. You can also serve it with sour cream. You might like to add some more fresh herbs for an even more delicious treat.

BREAD
AND
PASTRIES

This very tasty, very French, and very unusual dish is highly recommended. The special thing about recipes inspired by tarte tatin is the caramel that coats the fruit – or, in this case, the potatoes.

Potato tarte tatin

Vegetarian
Makes 1, 25cm
  (10in) diameter
Preparation 15 minutes
Cook 1 hour
Resting 5 minutes

800g (1¾lb) waxy potatoes
2 tbsp olive oil
50g (1¾oz) granulated sugar
50g (1¾oz) butter
3½ tbsp cider vinegar
2 tbsp soy sauce
100ml (3½fl oz) beer of
  your choice
a few sprigs of rosemary
4 garlic cloves
1 pack puff pastry, about
  250g (9oz), refrigerated
toasted sesame seeds
  for serving

Special equipment
25cm (10in) tart tin

Preheat the oven to 180°C (160°C fan/350°F/Gas 4). Peel the potatoes, cut into 1cm- (¹/₂in-) thick slices, transfer to a bowl, and toss in oil.

Scatter the sugar evenly over the tart tin and caramelize it over a moderate heat on the hob. As soon as it has turned golden, add the butter, vinegar, soy sauce, and beer. Be careful as it may splash. Bring everything to the boil without stirring and simmer gently until you have a smooth sauce. Lay the potatoes in a fan pattern in the tin and bake for 20 minutes.

Remove from the oven. The potatoes should be cooked but still with a bit of bite and the sauce should have cooked down to a syrup that is at least 5mm (¹/₄in) high in the tin. If the sauce is too thin, let it simmer down a bit more on the hob. If it is too thick, add a little more beer.

Wash the rosemary and shake dry. Set aside some as garnish, then strip the remaining needles and chop finely. Peel and finely chop the garlic. Sprinkle the chopped rosemary and garlic over the potatoes.

Trim the puff pastry sheet so it is slightly larger than the tin, prick with a fork, and lay it over the potatoes. Press the pastry down around the edges of the tin. Bake the tart in the oven for 25–30 minutes until golden brown.

Remove from the oven and leave to rest for 5 minutes, then turn the tart over onto a plate. Scatter with the reserved sprigs of rosemary and sesame seeds and serve immediately.

Wholemeal spelt flour gives this pastry a wonderfully intense, nutty flavour.
The tart also has the bonus of being rich in nutrients and fibre.

Potato and courgette tart

Vegetarian
Makes 1, 26cm
  (10¼in) diameter
Preparation 20 minutes
Chill 1½ hours
Cook 50 minutes

For the pastry
100g (3½oz) wholemeal
  spelt flour
200g (7oz) white spelt flour
1 pinch of salt
250g (9oz) fat-free quark
150g (5½oz) butter, plus
  extra for greasing

For the filling
400g (14oz) waxy or floury
  boiled potatoes
  (prepared previously)
2 medium courgettes
1 onion
1 garlic clove
100g (3½oz) pitted olives
a few sprigs thyme
½ bunch of parsley
olive oil for frying
salt and freshly ground
  black pepper
250ml (9fl oz) sour cream
2 eggs
100g (3½oz) grated Gruyère

Special equipment
26cm (10¼in) tart
  or springform tin

To make the pastry, combine both types of flour and the salt, then work in the quark and butter. Shape the pastry into a ball, wrap in clingfilm, and transfer to the fridge for at least 30 minutes.

Grease a tart or springform tin with butter. Roll the pastry out so it is slightly larger than the tin. Line the tin with the pastry, pressing it against the sides. Trim any excess pastry and prick the base with a fork. Chill the tin in the fridge for 1 hour.

Peel the potatoes for the filling and slice. Wash, trim, and slice the courgettes. Peel, halve, and finely slice the onion and garlic. Cut the olives into rings. Wash the thyme and parsley and shake dry. Strip the leaves and finely chop both herbs separately. Set the parsley aside.

Heat some oil in a large frying pan. Sauté the courgette, onion, and garlic until they are

beginning to brown, then season with salt and pepper. Stir in the thyme and olives and remove the pan from the hob.

Preheat the oven to 200°C (180°C fan/400°F/Gas 6). Whisk the sour cream and eggs, then season with salt and pepper. Remove the tin from the fridge and spread the sliced potatoes and the courgette mixture evenly over the pastry. Pour over the egg filling and sprinkle with grated cheese. Bake the tart for 40–45 minutes in the oven until golden brown and serve sprinkled with parsley.

Tip: this summer tart tastes just as good warm or cold, so it is the perfect thing to take on a picnic. Add a fresh salad and a glass of chilled rosé, and you have the perfect last-minute meal.

Some people are hesitant about making their own strudel dough.
But as long as the pastry is allowed to rest for long enough, it really
is very easy to stretch and work with. Why not give it a try?

Savoury potato and lentil strudel

Vegetarian
Serves 4
Preparation 30 minutes
Resting 30 minutes
Cook 1 hour 40 minutes

For the dough
150g (5½oz) flour, plus extra
    for working
1½ tbsp vegetable oil, plus
    extra for coating
½ tsp salt
50g (1¾oz) melted butter
    for brushing
1 tbsp breadcrumbs

For the filling
50g (1¾oz) beluga lentils
salt and freshly ground
    black pepper
2 large floury potatoes
2 garlic cloves
1 red pepper
2 spring onions
1 chilli
olive oil for frying
100g (3½oz) sauerkraut
honey for drizzling
100ml (3½fl oz) white wine

To make the dough, combine the flour, oil, salt, and 75ml (2¹/₂fl oz) lukewarm water, and work all the ingredients together to form a ball. Coat the dough with oil and wrap it in clingfilm or put it in a bowl covered with foil. Leave to rest at room temperature for 30 minutes.

To make the filling, boil the lentils in lightly salted water for 30 minutes, then drain. Meanwhile, peel the potatoes and boil in lightly salted water for 20–25 minutes until soft, then drain. Peel and finely chop the garlic. Wash the pepper, slice in half, remove the seeds and any white membrane, and cut into strips. Wash, trim, and slice the spring onions into rings. Wash the chilli, slice in half lengthways, remove the seeds if you prefer, and chop finely.

Heat some oil in a frying pan and sauté the garlic and pepper. Add the sauerkraut, spring onions, and chilli. Stir everything well, drizzle with honey, season with salt and pepper, and continue cooking for a few minutes, stirring constantly.

Deglaze the pan with wine and simmer the vegetables for 15 minutes, stirring frequently, until the liquid has almost completely boiled away. Then transfer the contents of the pan to a sieve and leave to drain. Crush the potatoes with a fork. Combine the potatoes, lentils, and other vegetables in a bowl. ▶

Roll the dough out to form a rectangle on a floured work surface. Slide your hands underneath the pastry, palms facing down, then gradually stretch the dough over the backs of your hands and then place it on a floured cloth. Trim off any thicker sections of pastry around the edges. Carefully brush melted butter over the pastry and sprinkle with breadcrumbs.

Preheat the oven to 200°C (180°C fan/400°F/Gas 6). Line a baking tray with baking paper. Put the filling on the lower third of the pastry, leaving 7–10cm (2^3/$_4$–4in) free around the edges.

Fold the left and right edges inwards, then roll up the pastry as tightly as possible using a tea towel to help you. Place it, seam side down, on the baking tray. Brush the strudel with melted butter and bake in the oven for 45–50 minutes. Brush twice more with butter while it is cooking and serve warm.

Tip: serve this strudel with some cream cheese or a yogurt dip. You could also make two smaller strudels instead of one large one. The small strudels will be ready after about 35–40 minutes in the oven.

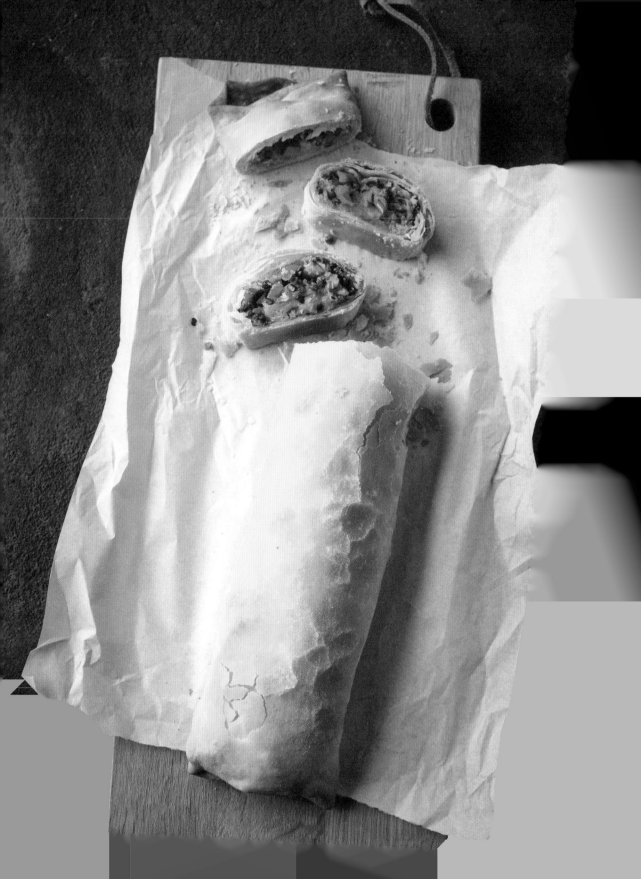

The very finest fusion cuisine, these Greek filo parcels are flavoured with soy sauce and served with a dip made from ajvar from Southern Europe, French crème fraîche, and fresh coriander, a herb that is popular in Asian recipes.

Filo parcels stuffed with potato and mince

Serves 5 as a starter
Preparation 25 minutes
Cook 25 minutes

For the parcels
1 onion
1 garlic clove
2 tbsp olive oil
250g (9oz) minced beef
2 boiled waxy or floury
    potatoes (either prepared
    previously or freshly
    cooked and cooled)
1 tsp dried oregano
1 tsp wholegrain mustard
2 tbsp soy sauce
salt and freshly ground
    black pepper
150g (5½oz) butter
5 sheets chilled filo pastry,
    30 × 30cm (12 x 12in)

For the dip
4 tbsp ajvar (roasted red
    pepper sauce), spicy or
    mild, as preferred
200ml (7fl oz) full-fat
    crème fraîche
1 bunch of coriander

Peel and dice the onion and garlic. Heat the oil in a frying pan and briskly fry the onion and garlic with the minced meat. Peel the potatoes, transfer them to a bowl, and roughly crush with a fork. Add the meat, oregano, mustard, and soy sauce, season with salt and pepper, and combine.

Preheat the oven to 200°C (180°C fan/400°F/Gas 6). Melt 50g (1³/₄oz) butter. Line a baking tray with baking paper. Brush the filo pastry with melted butter and cut each sheet lengthways into three strips. Spoon some of the filling on the bottom of each strip. Fold the lower left edge of the first strip diagonally up to the right over the filling. Then fold the bottom right corner diagonally up to the left. Keep folding diagonally in this way to the top of the strip. Repeat with the other strips until you have 15 triangular parcels. Place them on the baking tray.

Melt the remaining 100g (3¹/₂oz) butter and brush the parcels with it. Bake for 15–20 minutes in the oven until crisp.

To make the dip, combine the ajvar and crème fraîche and season with salt and pepper. Wash the coriander, shake dry, chop, and add to the dip. Serve with the filo parcels.

Alternative serving option: you can make a vegetarian version of these filo parcels by using 100g (3¹/₂oz) soy protein meat substitute. Soak this in 200ml (7fl oz) hot vegetable stock for 10 minutes, chop into fairly small pieces, and use instead of the mince.

Tip: filo pastry is easy to work with and produces a beautiful, flaky, crisp texture. It is important to brush the sheets with butter as quickly as possible to prevent them drying out.

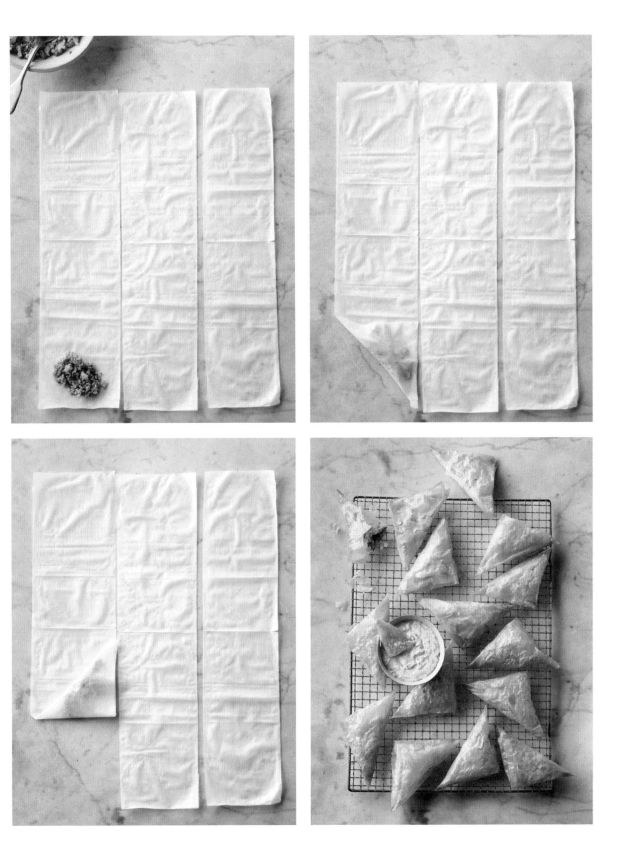

This is a simple tart, which conjures up a taste of France on your table. The potatoes come into direct contact with the tin, which helps them brown while they bake for a beautiful appearance and flavour.

Potato tart with garlic and herbs

Vegetarian
**Makes 1, 22cm
   (8¾in) diameter**
Preparation 25 minutes
Chill 30 minutes
Cook 45 minutes

For the pastry
100g (3½oz) cold butter, plus
   extra for greasing
100g (3½oz) full-fat
   cream cheese
200g (7oz) plain flour
½ tsp salt

For the topping
3–4 waxy potatoes
3 garlic cloves
1 sprig of rosemary
1 sprig of thyme
1 sprig of sage
100ml (3½fl oz) full-fat
   crème fraîche
2 eggs
1 tsp salt
3 tbsp olive oil
coarse sea salt and freshly
   ground black pepper

Special equipment
22cm (8¾in) tart tin

Grease a tart tin with butter. Rub the butter, cream cheese, flour, and salt together until the pastry has a smooth and elastic consistency. Roll out the pastry on a floured work surface until it is about 3cm (1¼in) larger than the tin. Line the tin with the pastry so it overlaps the edge. Press the pastry into position and prick all over with a fork, then trim off any excess pastry around the edge. Chill the pastry in the fridge for 30 minutes.

Wash and slice the potatoes, then immerse them in bowl of cold water. Preheat the oven to 200°C (180°C fan/400°F/ Gas 6). Peel and chop the garlic. Wash the herbs, shake dry, strip the leaves from the stalks, and chop.

Bake the pastry for 10 minutes to part-cook it, then remove from the oven. Lower the temperature to 180°C (160°C fan/350°F/

Gas 4). Combine the crème fraîche, eggs, garlic, two-thirds of the herbs, and season with 1 tsp salt. Spread this mixture over the pastry base and top with slices of potato in a fan shape. Brush the potatoes with oil and scatter over the remaining herbs. Bake the tart for 30–35 minutes in the oven, then remove from the oven and allow to cool slightly. Lift the tart out of the tin before slicing, and serve warm sprinkled with coarse sea salt and pepper.

Tip: you can replace the crème fraîche with a soft goat's cheese for a special flavour. If preferred, you can peel the potatoes before slicing. You can be very creative with the herbs. Choose your favourite or use whatever you happen to have growing.

This bread is not particularly time-consuming to make, but you will need to factor in the proving time because this is what makes the dough so moist and gives it such a great open texture. You can also make bread rolls with this recipe instead of a loaf.

Potato and spelt bread cooked in a cast-iron roasting dish

Vegan
Makes 1 loaf
Preparation 45 minutes
Resting 26 hours
Cook 1 hour 10 minutes

350g (12oz) floury potatoes
15g (½oz) salt, plus extra
    for cooking
200g (7oz) wholemeal
    spelt flour
200g (7oz) white spelt flour,
    plus extra for working
200g (7oz) spelt grains,
    crushed
½ tsp dried yeast

Special equipment
potato ricer
dough scraper
24cm (9½in) proving basket
    (optional)

Peel and chop the potatoes, then boil in lightly salted water for about 20–25 minutes until soft. Drain, leave to steam, then mash using a potato ricer. Leave to cool completely.

Combine both types of flour, the spelt grains, 15g (¹/₂oz) salt, and yeast in a bowl. Add 400ml (14fl oz) cold water and the potatoes, then mix everything thoroughly with a wooden spoon. Cover and leave the dough to prove for 24 hours at room temperature (about 20°C/68°F).

The next day, tip the dough out on a well-floured work surface and use a dough scraper to repeatedly fold the sides of the dough inwards. Dust the proving basket liberally with flour (or use a bowl lined with floured cotton cloth), place the dough inside, cover, and leave to prove for another 2 hours.

Put a lidded cast-iron roasting dish in the oven and heat it for

30 minutes to 260°C (240°C/ 500°F/Gas 10). Take the dish out of the oven, remove the lid, tip the bread upside down into the dish, and replace the lid. Lower the temperature to 220°C (200°C fan/425°F/Gas 7) and bake the bread for 30 minutes. Remove the lid and continue baking for 15 minutes. Take the bread out of the oven, place it on a wire rack, and leave to cool.

Tip: to make Swiss potato and seed bread rolls, prepare the dough as described above and add 100g (3¹/₂oz) sunflower seeds, 50g (1³/₄oz) each of linseed and pumpkin seeds, and 2 tsp crushed coriander seeds to the dough. Leave to prove overnight. The next day, preheat the oven to 230°C (210°C fan/ 450°F/Gas 8). Liberally dust the dough with flour. Use a spoon to scoop out large portions of dough and spread these over a lined baking tray. Irregular shapes are fine. Bake the bread rolls for about 20 minutes.

DESSERTS
AND CAKES

Plum dumplings are a popular dessert in many Eastern European countries. Traditionally, the plums are inside the dumplings, but here they are served alongside and have a rosemary and orange flavour.

Nut dumplings with rosemary-infused plums

Vegetarian
Serves 4
Preparation 20 minutes
Cook 55 minutes

For the plums
500g (1lb 2oz) plums, fresh
   or tinned
2 sprigs of rosemary
60g (2oz) brown sugar
zest and juice of 2
   organic oranges

For the dumplings
500g (1lb 2oz)
   floury potatoes
salt
50g (1¾oz) cornflour
2 egg yolks
60g (2oz) butter
2 tsp vanilla powder
50g (1¾oz) hazelnuts
2½ tbsp brown sugar
½ tsp ground cinnamon

Special equipment
potato ricer

Wash the fresh plums, if using, slice in half, and remove the stones. If using tinned, drain and remove the stones. Wash the rosemary, shake dry, strip the leaves from the stalks, and chop. Put the sugar in a saucepan and caramelize it over a moderate heat. Then add the orange juice. Next, add the rosemary and orange zest and simmer until the sugar has dissolved. Add the plums, cook them briefly, then remove from the pan. Simmer down the remaining liquid until it reaches a syrupy consistency. Take the pan off the heat and put the plums back in.

For the dumplings, wash the potatoes, then boil in lightly salted water for about 25–30 minutes until soft. Drain, peel immediately, and mash using a potato ricer. Sprinkle over the cornflour and add the egg yolks, 30g (1oz) butter, the vanilla powder, and a pinch of salt, then work all these ingredients together to make a dough.

Bring a large pan of salted water to the boil. Shape the dough into a roll and cut it into 8 equal pieces. Shape these into small dumplings, add to the hot water, and cook over a moderate heat for 8–10 minutes until they float to the surface.

Meanwhile, roughly chop the nuts. Melt the remaining 30g (1oz) butter in a pan. Add the nuts, sugar, and cinnamon and allow to brown. Remove the dumplings from the water using a slotted spoon, drain, and toss in the nutty butter. Serve with the warm or cold plums.

Tip: these potato dumplings make a delicious sweet main course. Roll them slightly smaller for a very special dessert.

In Bavaria, Schmarren are various desserts made from scrambled or shredded sweet items, the most famous example being Kaiserschmarren, or "Emperor's Mess", which is made from pieces of pancake. This potato Schmarren might be an indulgence, but it's worth it!

Bavarian potato Schmarren with raisins

Vegetarian
Serves 4
Preparation 20 minutes
Cook 55 minutes

300g (10oz) floury potatoes
salt
3 eggs
1 vanilla pod
100ml (3½fl oz) full-fat
    crème fraîche
70g (2¼oz) caster sugar
70g (2¼oz) raisins
1 tbsp butter
icing sugar for dusting

Special equipment
potato ricer

Preheat the oven to 180°C (160°C fan/350°F/Gas 4). Wash the potatoes and boil in lightly salted water for 25–30 minutes until soft. Drain, peel while still hot, and mash using a potato ricer. Separate the eggs. Slice the vanilla pod in half lengthways and scrape out the seeds. Mix the egg yolks, crème fraîche, vanilla seeds, and sugar into the mashed potato. Whisk the egg whites in a bowl until stiff, then immediately fold them into the potato mixture along with the raisins.

Heat the butter in an ovenproof dish, then add the potato mixture. Transfer the dish to the oven and bake for 20–25 minutes. Before serving, shred it with a fork and dust with icing sugar.

Tip: this dessert tastes best fresh from the oven. It goes beautifully with custard (see p182) or rosemary-infused plums (see p170). You might like to substitute cranberries instead of raisins.

This potato cake from the Saxony region of Germany is like a cross between stollen and another classic German recipe, the butter cake, which is a fairly plain traybake. The potato cake is also associated with a wonderful legend: because people were so impatient to tuck into their stollen, but this was strictly forbidden before the advent period, they would bake a cake "eked out" with potatoes, which they were then permitted to enjoy on the Sunday before advent (a religious holiday known as Totensonntag in Germany and Switzerland).

Saxon potato cake with cinnamon and sugar

Vegetarian
Makes 1
Preparation 25 minutes
Resting 45 minutes
Cook 55 minutes

For the dough
250g (9oz) floury potatoes
salt
600g (1lb 5oz) plain flour
1 sachet (7g/¼oz)
   dried yeast
140g (5oz) caster sugar
1 tsp vanilla powder
200ml (7fl oz) milk
125g (4½oz) soft butter
zest of 1 organic lemon
100g (3½oz) raisins
50g (1¾oz) chopped almonds

For the topping
100g (3½oz) butter
100g (3½oz) caster sugar
2 tsp ground cinnamon

Special equipment
potato ricer

Wash the potatoes, then boil in lightly salted water for about 25–30 minutes until soft. Drain, peel while still warm, and mash using a potato ricer. Mix the flour and yeast in a large bowl. Add the sugar, vanilla powder, milk, butter, lemon zest, and potatoes, and knead to make a dough. Leave to prove in a warm place for 20 minutes.

Work in the raisins and almonds, and leave the dough to prove for another 10 minutes. Line a baking tin with baking paper, roll the dough out on top and prick all over with a fork. Leave to prove for 15 minutes. Meanwhile, preheat the oven to 200°C (180°C fan/400°F/Gas 6).

Melt 50g (1¾oz) butter for the topping and brush this over the dough. Make small impressions in the dough and dot them with the remaining 50g (1¾oz) butter. Combine the sugar and cinnamon, scatter this over the dough, and bake in the oven for 20–25 minutes until golden.

Tip: cinnamon cream or vanilla ice cream taste delicious with this cake.

Savoury German potato noodles, or Schupfnudeln, have a sweet counterpart in the form of Mohnnudeln, which are made from potatoes and poppy seeds. In summer, these taste great with baked apricots; in autumn, plums with cinnamon make a great companion; and in winter, you can't go wrong with a baked apple compote.

Potato noodles with poppy seeds and baked apricots

Vegetarian
Serves 4
Preparation 25 minutes
Cook 1 hour

For the noodles
600g (1lb 5oz)
    floury potatoes
salt
100g (3½oz) butter
2 egg yolks
175g (6oz) plain flour, plus
    extra for working
1 pinch of grated nutmeg
2 tbsp ground poppy seeds
icing sugar for dusting

For the apricots
½ vanilla pod
500g (1lb 2oz) apricots
2 star anise
3 cardamom pods
1 cinnamon stick
2 tbsp maple syrup
200ml (7fl oz) white wine
    or white grape juice
zest strips and juice of
    1 organic lemon

Special equipment
potato ricer

Wash the potatoes, then boil in lightly salted water for about 25–30 minutes until soft. Meanwhile, preheat the oven to 160°C (140°C fan/325°F/Gas 3).

To prepare the apricots, first slice the vanilla pod in half lengthways, scrape out the seeds, and discard the pod. Wash the apricots, slice them in half, and remove the stones. Then transfer to an ovenproof dish with the spices, maple syrup, wine, and lemon zest and juice. Bake in the oven for 15–20 minutes.

Drain the potatoes, peel, and mash using a potato ricer. Add 25g (scant 1oz) butter, the egg yolks, flour, 2 pinches of salt, and nutmeg, then quickly work all the ingredients together to make a dough. Shape the dough into a roll on a well-floured work surface, divide into pieces, and use your hands to roll them into finger-length noodles.

Bring plenty of lightly salted water in a saucepan to a simmer. Add the potato noodles to the pan, bring to the boil, and boil for 5 minutes. Drain the cooked noodles in a sieve. Put the remaining 75g (2¹/₂oz) butter in a frying pan and heat until it is foaming and golden brown. Add the poppy seeds and toss the noodles in this mixture.

Dust the potato noodles with icing sugar and serve with the apricots.

Tip: instead of apricots, you could also try baked peaches or nectarines.

Semolina dumplings, or Grießnocken, are an Austrian speciality and the perfect treat for children. Adding potatoes to the mixture makes them even lighter. Serve with blueberry compote and everyone will be happy.

Potato and semolina dumplings with cinnamon and sugar

Vegetarian
Serves 4
Preparation 20 minutes
Cook 40 minutes

200g (7oz) floury potatoes
salt
½ vanilla pod
250ml (9fl oz) almond milk
4 tbsp golden caster sugar
zest of ½ organic orange
zest of ½ organic lemon
75g (2½oz) semolina
1 egg
30g (1oz) butter
2 tsp ground cinnamon

Special equipment
potato ricer

Peel and chop the potatoes, then boil in lightly salted water for about 20–25 minutes until soft. Meanwhile, slice the vanilla pod in half lengthways and scrape out the seeds. Add the almond milk, 1 tbsp sugar, a pinch of salt, the orange and lemon zest, and the vanilla seeds to a saucepan, and bring to the boil. Pour in the semolina and return to the boil, stirring constantly. Then simmer for 5 minutes over a very low heat, stirring occasionally. Remove from the hob and leave to cool until lukewarm.

Drain the potatoes and leave to steam for 1 minute on the hob with the heat turned off. Heat some lightly salted water in another pan to a simmer. Mash the potatoes using a ricer and add to the semolina mixture. Add the egg and butter and stir well.

Use two spoons to scoop out dollops of the mixture and cook them in the simmering water for 10 minutes. Combine the remaining 3 tbsp sugar with the cinnamon. Arrange the dumplings on plates and serve with the cinnamon sugar.

Tip: a quick blueberry compote tastes fantastic with these dumplings: mix 250g (9oz) frozen blueberries in a saucepan with 2 tsp cornflour, bring to the boil, stirring constantly, and simmer for 1–2 minutes. Add a combination of lemon juice and sugar or honey to the compote to taste. Leave to cool and serve with the dumplings.

Sweetened potato fritters with rosemary-infused cherries

Vegetarian
Serves 4
Preparation 20 minutes
Cook 15 minutes

For the compote
½ organic lemon
2 sprigs of rosemary
3 tbsp caster sugar
300g (10oz) frozen
   cherries, defrosted
1 heaped tsp cornflour

For the fritters
600g (1lb 5oz)
   floury potatoes
2 tbsp flour
1 egg
salt
4 tbsp neutral-tasting
   cooking oil for frying
icing sugar (optional)

To make the compote, wash the lemon and dab dry, then peel off 2 strips of zest. Wash the rosemary and shake dry.

Caramelize the sugar slightly in a saucepan over a moderate heat. Add the rosemary and lemon zest and heat briefly. Add the cherries, including their defrosted juice, and 100ml (3¹/₂fl oz) water, then simmer for 5 minutes. Stir the cornflour into 2 tbsp water to make a paste, add it to the cherries, and continue cooking the compote for 1 minute, stirring constantly. Set it aside to cool.

To make the fritters, peel and finely grate the potatoes and squeeze out as much liquid as possible. Combine the grated potato with the flour, egg, and a pinch of salt. Heat the oil in a large frying pan. Use a soup spoon to scoop dollops of the potato mixture into the hot oil, frying each one on both sides until golden brown.

Drain the fritters on kitchen towel, dust with icing sugar, if using, and serve with the cherries.

Tip: if you prefer your fritters slightly sweeter, you could add some icing sugar to the batter. Other spices such as cinnamon make a great addition to the mixture, as do lemon or orange zest and vanilla.

Steamed potato pudding with custard and grapes

Vegetarian
Serves 6
Preparation 25 minutes
Cook 1 hour 25 minutes

For the pudding
butter for greasing
3 tbsp breadcrumbs
500g (1lb 2oz)
    floury potatoes
salt
100g (3½oz) ground
    hazelnuts
3 eggs, separated
75g (2½oz) caster sugar
100ml (3½fl oz) milk

For the custard
1 vanilla pod
1 egg yolk
25g (scant 1oz) cornflour
2–3 tbsp caster sugar
400ml (14fl oz) milk
100ml (3½fl oz) single cream

250g (9oz) black grapes
juice of ½ lemon
1 tbsp cherry jam
icing sugar for dusting
3 sprigs of fresh mint
    (optional)

Special equipment
20cm (8in) pudding basin
    with lid
potato ricer

Grease the pudding basin with butter and sprinkle with breadcrumbs. Peel and chop the potatoes, then boil in lightly salted water for about 20–25 minutes until soft. Toast the nuts in a pan over a moderate heat.

Drain the potatoes and leave to steam on the hob for about 1 minute with the heat turned off. Whisk the egg whites with a pinch of salt until stiff. Beat the egg yolks and sugar together in a separate bowl until creamy. Mash the potatoes using a ricer and stir in the milk. Mix the potatoes and nuts into the beaten egg-yolk mixture, then gently fold in the whisked egg whites. Transfer to the pudding basin and put the lid on.

Pour 3cm (1¼in) water into a large saucepan that can accommodate your pudding basin. Put a saucer or stainless steel ring in the pan to stop the basin touching the bottom of the pan and put the basin on top. Cover the saucepan with a lid and steam the pudding for 1 hour, checking the water level occasionally and topping up with boiling water if necessary.

To make the custard, slice the vanilla pod in half lengthways and scrape out the seeds. Combine the egg yolk, cornflour, vanilla seeds, and sugar. Put the milk, cream, and vanilla pod in a saucepan and bring to the boil, then add the egg-yolk mixture. Return to boiling point and simmer for 1 minute, stirring constantly. Transfer to a jug or other suitable container, cover, and leave to cool. Remove the vanilla pod before serving.

Wash the grapes, remove the stalks, slice in half, and combine with the lemon juice and jam. Lift the pudding basin out of the saucepan and remove the lid. Turn out the pudding, dust with icing sugar, slice into portions, and serve with the grapes and custard. Garnish with mint leaves, if using.

This is a quick recipe that should be served and enjoyed immediately: because of the whisked egg whites, soufflés soon collapse and lose their fluffy consistency.

Potato soufflés with vanilla pears

Vegetarian
Serves 4–6
Preparation 20 minutes
Cook 55 minutes
Marinating overnight

For the pears
3 firm pears
juice of 1 lemon
1 vanilla pod
50g (1¾oz) granulated sugar
150ml (5fl oz) white wine

For the soufflés
25g (scant 1oz) butter, plus
    extra for greasing
50g (1¾oz) raw cane
    sugar, plus extra for
    the ramekins
200g (7oz) floury potatoes
100ml (3½fl oz) sour cream
4 eggs
salt
1 tsp ground cinnamon
2 tsp cornflour
icing sugar for dusting
    (optional)

Special equipment
4–6 ovenproof ramekins

Wash, halve, and core the pears. Transfer to a bowl and toss in the lemon juice. Slice the vanilla pod in half lengthways and scrape out the seeds. Caramelize the sugar in a large pan over a moderate heat, then add the wine. Add the pears and lemon juice, vanilla seeds and pod, then simmer for 5 minutes. Remove from the hob and leave the fruit to infuse in the liquid overnight.

Grease the ramekins with butter and sprinkle with sugar. Peel and chop the potatoes, then boil in lightly salted water for about 20–25 minutes until soft. Drain the potatoes and leave them to steam on the hob with the heat turned off. Meanwhile, preheat the oven to 180°C (160°C fan/350°F/Gas 4). Mash the potatoes using a potato masher and leave to cool until lukewarm. Stir in the butter and sour cream.

Separate the eggs. Whisk the egg yolks with the sugar until thick and creamy. Whisk the egg whites with a pinch of salt until stiff. Mix the potatoes, cinnamon, and cornflour into the whisked egg yolks. Gently fold in the whisked egg whites and transfer the mixture into the prepared ramekins. Line an ovenproof dish with a layer of kitchen towel, place the ramekins inside, and pour in boiling water to about halfway up the dish. Bake the soufflés in the oven for 20 minutes.

Remove the soufflés from the oven, dust with icing sugar, if using, and serve immediately with the pears.

Index

Acknowledgments

DK would like to thank Amber Dalton for consultancy,
Eloise Grohs for design assistance, and John Friend
for proofreading.

Additional photography
Stuart West Photography Ltd for photography,
XAB Design for photography art direction,
and Jane Lawrie for food styling.

DK LONDON
Translator Alison Tunley
Senior Editor Dawn Titmus
Editor Lucy Philpott
Senior Designer Glenda Fisher
Senior Acquisitions Editor Stephanie Milner
Design Manager Marianne Markham
Production Editor David Almond
Production Controller Rebecca Parton
Jacket Designer Amy Cox
Jacket Coordinator Jasmin Lennie
Art Director Maxine Pedliham
Publishing Director Katie Cowan

DK DELHI
DTP Designer Manish Upreti
Pre-production Manager Sunil Sharma
Index Hina Jain

DK GERMANY
Recipes, text, and photographs Manuela Rüther
Food and other styling Agnes Prus and Bettina Bormann
Editorial Anja Ashauer-Schupp
Typesetting Martin Feuerstein, Munich
Programme Management Monika Schlitzer
Editorial Management Marline Ernzer
Project Support Julia Sommer
Production Management Dorothee Whittaker
Production Control Arnika Marx
Production Inga Reinke

First published in Great Britain in 2022 by
Dorling Kindersley Limited
DK, One Embassy Gardens, 8 Viaduct Gardens,
London, SW11 7BW

The authorized representative in the EEA is
Dorling Kindersley Verlag GmbH. Arnulfstr. 124,
80636 Munich, Germany

A CIP catalogue record for this book
is available from the British Library.
ISBN: 978-0-2415-8063-9

Printed and bound in China

For the curious
www.dk.com

NOTES
Recipes: the butter used in the recipes
is unsalted.

The information and suggestions in this book
have been carefully considered and checked
by the authors and publisher; however, no
guarantee is assumed. Neither the author nor
the publisher and its representatives are liable
for any personal, material, or financial damage.

This book was made with Forest
Stewardship Council™ certified
paper – one small step in DK's
commitment to a sustainable future.
For more information go to
www.dk.com/our-green-pledge